Words Their Way

Word Sorts for Within Word Pattern Spellers

Marcia Invernizzi
University of Virginia

Francine Johnston
University of North Carolina, Greensboro

Donald R. Bear
University of Nevada, Reno

PEARSON
Merrill
Prentice Hall

Upper Saddle River, New Jersey
Columbus, Ohio

Library of Congress Cataloging-in-Publication Data

Words their way : word sorts for within word pattern spellers / Marcia Invernizzi ... [et al.]. — 1st ed.

   p. cm.
   ISBN 0-13-183816-4
   1. English language—Orthography and spelling—Problems, exercises, etc. I. Invernizzi, Marcia.

PE1145.2.W67 2004
428.1—dc21

2003052713

Vice President and Executive Publisher: Jeffery W. Johnston
Senior Editor: Linda Ashe Montgomery
Editorial Assistant: Laura Weaver
Development Editor: Hope Madden
Production Editor: Mary M. Irvin
Production Coordination: Amy Gehl, Carlisle Publishers Services
Design Coordinator: Diane C. Lorenzo
Cover Designer: Ali Mohrman
Cover Image: Jean Claude Lejuene
Production Manager: Pamela D. Bennett
Director of Marketing: Ann Castel Davis
Marketing Manager: Darcy Betts Prybella
Marketing Coordinator: Tyra Poole
Illustrator: Francine R. Johnston

This book was set in Palatino by Carlisle Communications, Ltd. It was printed and bound by Phoenix Color Corp. The cover was printed by Phoenix Color Corp.

Pearson Education Ltd.
Pearson Education Singapore Pte. Ltd.
Pearson Education Canada, Ltd.
Pearson Education—Japan

Pearson Education Australia Pty. Limited
Pearson Education North Asia Ltd.
Pearson Educación de Mexico, S.A. de C.V.
Pearson Education Malaysia Pte. Ltd.

10 9 8 7 6 5 4 3 2 1
ISBN: 0-13-183816-4

Preface

Words Their Way: Word Sorts for Within Word Pattern Spellers is intended to supplement the text *Words Their Way: Word Study for Phonics, Vocabulary, and Spelling Instruction*. That core text provides a practical, research-based, and classroom-proven way to study words with students. This supplemental text expands and enriches that word study, specifically for within word pattern spellers.

Within word pattern spellers are typically transitional readers. During this stage of development, students learn to spell long-vowel patterns, and they read most single-syllable words accurately and with increasing fluency. They are ready to begin contrasting long and short vowels, and sorting words by grammatic and semantic features.

Words Their Way: Word Sorts for Within Word Pattern Spellers provides teachers with prepared reproducible sorts and step-by-step directions on how to guide students through the sorting lesson. There are organizational tips as well as follow-up activities to extend the lesson through weekly routines. The materials provided in this text will complement the use of any existing phonics, spelling, and reading curricula.

More resources for word study in the within word pattern stage, including additional spelling inventories for grades 1 through 4, resources for using word study with students who speak Spanish, links to websites related to word study, as well as news about the *Words Their Way* CD-ROM and Video, and other companion materials and word study events, can be found on the text's Companion Website. You can link to this site at

www.prenhall.com/bear

Contents

Overview

This collection of sorts includes both pictures and words for students who are in the early-to-late within word pattern stage of spelling. These students are usually in the late first to mid-fourth grades and should already know how to hear and spell two-letter consonant blends and digraphs, as well as short vowels, to be ready for the features in this book. To figure out exactly where individual students should start within this supplement, you need to administer one of the spelling inventories and use the feature guides in Chapter 2 of *Words Their Way*.

Research shows that students are using but confusing all of the long-vowel patterns at about the same time, so there is some interplay in the sequence presented here among the vowels. Short (lax)- and long (tense)-vowel sounds are introduced first with pictures, and then the patterns are covered using words. Common and less common long-vowel patterns are then revisited in *r*-influenced contrasts and include homophones—words that sound the same but are spelled with different patterns to reflect different meanings (e.g., *pair* and *pear*). Students then focus on vowel diphthongs and other ambiguous vowel patterns that reflect a range of vowel sounds that are neither long nor short—sounds like the glided vowel in the middle of *boil* or *noise.* Complex consonant patterns such as the *tch* in the words *match* or *scotch* and other consonant patterns that are influenced by vowel sounds are examined in sorts that build on concepts developed in the earlier sorts. At the same time we expand the repertoire of consonant clusters to include more difficult three-letter digraphs and blends. Silent consonants found at the beginning of words are introduced at this time as well. We start examining two-syllable words toward the end of this sequence by categorizing two-syllable high-frequency words. Finally, there is a brief introduction to inflectional word endings with the past-tense morpheme (*-ed*) and plurals. These round off the within word pattern stage and segue into the next *Words Their Way* word sort book, syllables and affixes. The grand finale of this book of sorts is a review of all the long-vowel patterns through the study of homophones.

For each set of sorts there are *Notes for the Teacher* and suggestions to introduce and practice the sort. Sorts are presented as black line masters that can be reproduced for every student. We recommend that you enlarge the sorts about 10% to maximize the paper size. It is important that students sort their own words several times. You should also use the masters to prepare a set of pictures and words for modeling. You may want to make a transparency of the sort and cut it apart for use on an overhead or enlarge the words for use in a pocket chart. You can also simply make your own copy to cut apart and use on a desktop or on the floor.

Most of the sorting lessons are described as teacher-directed closed sorts with pre-established categories indicated with headers and key words. For more discovery-oriented lessons you can cut off the headers before duplicating the sorts and encourage your students to establish their own categories in an open sort. Headers might then be used to label the columns. The Appendix contains a variety of headers that you can use to label your categories. See Chapters 3 and 6 of *Words Their Way* (WTW) and the *Words Their Way* CD-ROM (*WTWCD*) for additional background information, organizational tips, games, and activities. Use the Independent Word Study form in the Appendix for homework.

The pacing for these sorts is designed for slow to average growth and the words selected for the sorts are the most frequently occuring words for that sound or pattern. The bolded key words are number one in frequency. After introducing a sort, you should spend about a week following routines that encourage students to practice for mastery. However, if your students seem to be catching on quickly you can speed up the pace by spending fewer days on a sort or you may skip some sorts altogether. However, you may need to slow down and perhaps even create additional sorts for some students using the blank template in the Appendix. More difficult words are included for each sort to provide more practice or to challenge students with a more developed reading vocabulary; these words are bolded in the word list in the Appendix. Additional words may be found in the Appendix of *Words Their Way* (WTW).

Marcia Invernizzi
Francine Johnston
Donald Bear

SORTS 1-6

Picture Sorts for Short- and Long-Vowel Sounds

NOTES FOR THE TEACHER

These first six picture sorts are designed to focus students' attention on the vowel sound in the middle of single-syllable words and to provide ample practice in recognizing, identifying, and categorizing vowel sounds as either long or short. Direct instruction in segmenting and isolating the vowel sound in the middle of single-syllable words lays the phonological foundation for learning how to spell long-vowel patterns.

Some students may think that the terms *long* and *short* refer to the height or length of the letters on the page. Be sure they understand that the term *long vowel* refers to the *sound* of the vowel.

Directly teaching vowel sounds with pictures is especially useful for students in the early within word pattern stage. If you see that students have missed only one or two long-vowel patterns on a spelling inventory and are representing most long-vowel patterns correctly in their writing, then you will want to skip to later sorts in this book. You may also want to use the first Spell Check for a pretest to see which students will require instruction in isolating the medial vowel sound. Additional review will take place as students work with words in the next section.

The first six picture sorts can be used with students who have mastered the spelling of most two-letter consonant digraphs and blends at the beginning and end of words and correctly represent most short-vowel sounds in the middle. With these basic phonics features under their belt, students begin to "use but confuse" silent vowels that provide the signal that a vowel sound is long, often spelling words like *snake* as SNAIK. Typically these children are in late first or second grade. Students should begin their study of long-vowel patterns by comparing and contrasting short- and long-vowel sounds in single-syllable words.

The pictures in sorts 1–6 represent words that are already in most students' oral vocabulary. English Language Learners (ELLs) may learn new words by working collaboratively with a buddy who names each picture as it is sorted. Key pictures are provided to associate with each sound and these should be placed at the top of each column to explicitly label the category. The key pictures contain key words and highlight the vowel under study (see the Appendix in *WTW* for sound boards containing the key words and pictures used throughout this supplement). While working with picture sorts, children will practice phoneme segmentation skills as they learn to divide each word into its individual sounds. When phoneme segmentation is difficult, students should be encouraged to peel away the consonant sounds at the beginning and end of the word to isolate the vowel sound in the middle. For example, if students are having difficulty segmenting the word *rain* into three individual phonemes, try having them say *rain* without the /r/ sound (*ain*); and then *ain* without the /n/ sound.

Five picture sorts in this section feature one-syllable words for each of the five vowels. Each sort focuses on one vowel at a time and includes words that contain both short- and long-vowel sounds. Each sort also contains an oddball (e.g. *foot* in sort #1).The sixth sort contrasts short- and long-vowel sounds of all five vowels. Since these six introductory sorts are so similar, you may be able to introduce and practice three picture sorts per week. Students who find it difficult to isolate the medial vowel sound will need a slower, more explicit presentation. To make these sorts even more explicit, ask students to segment and count the individual sounds within a few words in each category. For example, after sorting the picture of the *slide* under the key picture/word for the long *-i* sound (*kite*), you may ask students to count the four sounds in the word *slide*, perhaps by pushing a counter for each sound. After deconstructing the sounds within the word, students should blend the sounds together again to reconstruct it (e.g., /s/ + /l/ + /i/ + /d/ = *slide*).

When possible, share books that contain a number of words with the same vowel sounds being studied. For example, *The Cake That Jake Baked* is a natural connection to the long *-a* sound, while *Sheep in a Jeep* plays on the long *-e*. You may also have poems, rhymes, or traditional chants that feature short- and long-vowel sounds, such as *Old Hogan's Goat* in *Juba This and Juba That* (Tashjian, 1969). You might present these on a chart or overhead and underline target words before or after doing the sorting activities.

STANDARD WEEKLY ROUTINES FOR USE WITH SORTS 1–6

1. **Repeated Work with the Pictures:** Students should repeat the sort several times after it has been modeled and discussed under the teacher's direction. After cutting out the pictures and using them for individual practice, the pieces can be stored in an envelope or baggie to sort again several times on other days. See *WTW* (Chapter 3) for tips on managing picture sorting.

2. **Draw and Label and Cut and Paste:** For seat work, students can draw additional pictures of words containing the targeted vowel sounds. They can also look for pictures in magazines and catalogs and paste those into categories according to the medial vowel sound. The pictures from the black line sort can be pasted into categories and children can be asked to label them. Or, the pictures from this sort can be reduced in size and glued onto paper in columns. This can serve as an assessment tool but *do not* expect accurate spelling of the entire word at this time.

3. **Games and Other Activities:** Many games are described in *WTW* and are available to print out from the *WTW* CD-ROM. Variations of the Follow-the-Path game work especially well for short- and long-vowel sounds. You might want to create one for each of the first five sorts presented here.

SORTS 1–6   SHORT- AND LONG-VOWEL SOUNDS
Demonstrate, Sort, Check, and Reflect

1. Prepare a set of pictures to use for teacher-directed modeling. Use the key pictures as headers and display the pictures randomly, picture side up.
2. Begin a sound sort by modeling one picture into each column, **demonstrating** and explaining explicitly what you are doing. Model by stretching out the vowel sound in the middle to emphasize its sound: *Here is a picture of rain. . . Rrr—$\overline{aaaa}$—nn; I hear the letter A say its name in the middle. When we hear a vowel say its name in the middle, we call it a long-vowel sound. I hear a long -a in the middle of rain, so I will put it under the picture of the cake. This is a picture of a bag. Bb—aaa—gg has a short -a in the middle—the /a/ sound like in the middle of the word* cat. *I'll put bag under cat because they both have the /a/ sound, the short -a sound in the middle. Now who can help me sort the rest of these pictures?* Continue with the children's help to **sort** all of the pictures. Model how to divide words into individual phonemes to isolate, identify, and then categorize the medial vowel sound in each word. When all the pictures have been sorted, **check** the sort. Name all of the pictures in each column and check to make sure they all have the same vowel sound in the middle. *Do all of these sound alike in the middle? Do we need to move any?* Be sure to model the discovery and placement of the oddball.
3. Repeat the sort with the group again. Keep the key pictures and the letter as headers. You may want to mix up the pictures and turn them face down in a deck this time and let children take turns drawing a card and sorting it in the correct column. You can also simply pass out the pictures and have the children take turns sorting them. After sorting, model how to check by naming the words in each column and then **reflect** about how the words in each column are alike. Talk about how the words in each column are alike and how they are different from the words in the other column. Now would be the time to discuss oddballs or any other words that were difficult to categorize and why. Oddballs include *foot* (sort #1), *net* (sort #2), *vase* (sort #3), *cake* (sort #4), and *fork* (sort #5).
4. **Extend.** Give each student a copy of the sort for individual practice. Enlarge the sort sheet by 10% before copying to eliminate the border. Assign the students the task of cutting out the pictures to sort on their own in the same way they did in the group. As they sort independently, ask individual students about how they are sorting and why they placed a particular picture in a column. Ask them to tell you what sounds they are working on. Give each student a plastic bag or envelope to store the pieces. On subsequent days students should repeat the sorting activity several times. Involve the students in the other weekly routines listed above and described in *WTW* for the within word pattern stage. The *WTW* CD-ROM has additional picture sorts with matching words that work with these same sounds.

   Notes for Sort 6: Sort 6 provides a transition to the next set of sorts where students will sort just words. There is no pattern in this sort—just have your students listen for the sound of the vowel. Lay down the headers for each long-vowel sound, then sort the pictures by the vowel sounds in the middle. After checking the placement of the pictures, match each word card to its corresponding picture.

SORT 1 Picture Sort for Long and Short -a

ă 🐈	ā 🥫	*oddball*	

SORT 2   Picture Sort for Long and Short -*i*

ĭ 🐷	ī 🪁	oddball	

Words Their Way: Word Sorts for Within Word Pattern Spellers © 2004 by Prentice-Hall, Inc.

SORT 3   Picture Sort for Long and Short -o

ŏ 🦴	ō 🧦	oddball	

SORT 4   Picture Sort for Long and Short -*u*

ŭ 🍵	ū 🧦	*oddball*	
(glue)	(rug)	(jacket)	(hand)
(spoon)	(donkey)	(tub)	(bug)
(moon)	(truck)	(shoe)	(plug)
(cake)	(sun)	(drum)	(fruit)
(roof)	(elephant)	(spearmint)	(nut)

Words Their Way: Word Sorts for Within Word Pattern Spellers © 2004 by Prentice-Hall, Inc.

SORT 5   Picture Sort for Long and Short -*e*

ĕ 🛏	ē 🧦	oddball	

SORT 6   Review of Long Vowels with Word Matches

ā 🍰 cake	ē 👣 feet	ī 🪁 kite	ō 🦴 bone
ū 🧦 tube	tape	bike	cone
cube	bee	cane	bride
rose	flute	three	snake

Words Their Way: Word Sorts for Within Word Pattern Spellers © 2004 by Prentice-Hall, Inc.

Word Sorts Contrasting Short- and Long-Vowel Sounds and Patterns (CVC and CVCe)

NOTES FOR THE TEACHER

Most students easily notice that adding a silent *-e* to the end of a short-vowel word makes the vowel say its name. They see that the addition of the silent *-e* changes the short-vowel sound into a long-vowel sound: *tap* becomes *tape; can* becomes *cane; cub* becomes *cube.* While the initial use of pictures in the first six sorts helped your students discriminate the two vowel sounds, only by examining printed words will your students learn to associate the CVCe pattern with the long-vowel sound. The silent *-e,* or CVCe pattern, is the most common long-vowel spelling for *a, i, o,* and *u.* In single-syllable words, the CVCe pattern does not occur often for *e,* so the long-vowel spellings of *e* are not included here. The few spelling patterns for *e* may be found in the next set of sorts (13–18) that examine other long-vowel patterns.

Sorts 7–12 are designed for students in the early within word pattern stage who are just learning to associate the CVCe pattern with the long-vowel sounds for *a, i, o,* and *u.* Most of the words in these sorts are on a late first- and second-grade level. More difficult words that follow the same pattern are also provided for each sort. Make sure your students can read the words in each sort. You might use the Spell Check on page 28 as a pretest to see which of your students are in need of these particular sorts. Students who spell most of the words on the Spell Check correctly may benefit from the study of other common long-vowel patterns in the next section. Different pacing schemes for the within word pattern stage are suggested in *WTW.*

Although you want your students to use spelling patterns to help them read and spell, you do not want them to overrely on visual cues to the exclusion of the sound they represent. The silent *-e* at the end of words proffers a strong visual pull. If the pattern-to-sound association is not firmly established, they may not be able to spell without copying from a word card or some other visual crutch while writing.

In sorts 7–12 we take several measures to offset the strong draw to the visual at the expense of the sound. First, we include several pictures with each word sort in this section to induce students to categorize by sound as well as by pattern. Second, we recommend the use of blind or no-peeking sorts as a standard weekly routine. No-peeking sorts require students to categorize a word by sound before they see its spelling pattern.

Third, we incorporate oddballs that violate the prevailing pattern-to-sound correspondence. High-frequency words like *come, some, done,* and *have* are also incorporated to keep your students on their toes. These words are spelled with the CVCe pattern but do not have the long-vowel sound. For more information on blind or no-peeking sorts and on dealing with high-frequency words, see Chapter 6 of *WTW*.

Sorts 7–10 require students to categorize words and pictures by short- or long-vowel sounds. The same key words and pictures that were used to head the categories in sorts 1–6 are used again here. Each sort contains at least one oddball, a word that follows the pattern for a particular vowel sound but does not contain that vowel sound. Students should be encouraged to find "the odd one out" after they sort and to articulate why it does not fit into either category by sound or by pattern.

Sort 11 requires students to categorize short- and long-vowel sounds and patterns across all four vowels. Sort 12 focuses on the spelling of words ending in *ck, ke,* or *k,* and demonstrates how these word endings are also tied directly to the vowel sounds.

When possible, share books that contain a number of words from the targeted vowel sounds as a way to introduce or reinforce the pattern-to-sound consistency. For example, *Make Way for Ducklings* (McCloskey, 1941) is a natural connection for the *ck* versus *ke* and *k* distinctions presented in sort 12 since the ducklings' names are Jack, Kack, Lack, Mack, Nack, Ouack, Pack, and Quack. You may also have poems or chants that feature similar short- and long-vowel sounds and patterns such as *Seven Little Rabbits* (Tashijian, 1941), that feature many long-vowel sounds. You might present these on a chart or overhead and underline target words before or after doing the sorting and activities.

STANDARD WEEKLY ROUTINES
FOR USE WITH SORTS 7–12

1. **Repeated Work with the Pictures and Words:** Students should work with the featured sorts several times after the sort has been modeled and discussed, as described in each lesson below. After cutting out the words and pictures, the pieces can be stored in an envelope or baggie to be sorted again for individual practice on other days. The pictures and words can also be used in partner activities where students work together to read and spell the words. At some point students may glue down the sort or they may keep it to combine with additional sorts in review lessons.

2. **Writing Sorts and Word Study Notebooks:** Students should record their word sorts by writing them into columns in their notebooks under the same key words and pictures that headed the columns of their word sort. Writing their sorts into columns gives students practice with writing the word and provides a "home base" for the other weekly routines and homework assignments. At the bottom of the writing sort, have your students **reflect** on what they learned in that particular sort and write their observations about the spelling of certain sounds. See Chapter 3 in *WTW* for more detailed descriptions of word study notebooks.

3. **Change-O:** This activity is especially appropriate for early within word pattern spellers. Choose four or five words to work with, then show students how they can change a letter to make a new word. Typically, consonants are exchanged for other consonants at the beginning (*make-bake*) or end (*mad-mat*) of words. Consonant blends may be exchanged for other consonant blends as well (*grass-class*), or digraphs for digraphs (*chin-thin*) at either the beginning or end of words (*wish-with*). As students progress further through this stage, see if they can change the vowel in the middle to come up with a new word (*drive-drove; give-gave*) and have them write their new creations in their word study notebooks.

4. **Word Hunts:** Students can look for words in daily reading that mirror the featured sound or pattern. Challenge children to find others that contain the same vowel

sound and/or pattern; or brainstorm additional words. After they find examples of the sound or pattern they are looking for, they can add the words to the bottom of the proper column in their word study notebook. You may want to create posters or displays of all the words students can discover for each category.

5. **Dictated Sentences:** Tell your students that you study patterns that go with short- and long-vowel sounds so that they can read and spell. Prepare a sentence that contains several of your word study words. Read the sentence to your students and have them write it. Give them feedback about their spelling and mechanics.

6. **Blind or No-Peeking Sorts and No-Peeking Writing Sorts:** A blind or no-peeking sort should only be done after students have had a chance to practice a word sort several times. Key words are laid down as headers. Students work together and take turns calling out a word without showing it. The other student points to where the word should go and the partner then shows the word card to check its spelling against the key word. In a blind or no-peeking writing sort, key words are written at the top of a sheet of paper. The student then writes the words in the correct column as they are called aloud. After the word has been written, the partner calling the words shows the word card to the student doing the writing to check for correctness. No-peeking sorts require students to think about words by sound and by pattern and to use the key words as models for analogy. Buddy sorts like the blind or no-peeking sorts are a great way to practice for spelling tests and can be assigned for homework. See the homework form in the Appendix.

7. **Games and Other Activities:** Create games and activities such as those in *WTW* or download them ready made from the *WTW* CD-ROM. The Train Station game is one we highly recommend for use with all long-vowel patterns. Other games, such as Green Light! Red Light!, Scattergories, Word Study Trivial Pursuit, and UNO, are described in Chapter 6 of *WTW*.

8. **Assessment:** To assess students' weekly mastery, ask them to both spell and read the words. An assessment of all the short- and long (CVCe pattern)-vowel words used in these sorts follows the sorts on page 28: Spell Check 1: Short versus Long (CVCe).

SORT 7   SHORT -A VERSUS LONG -A (CVCe)

Prepare a set of pictures and words to use for teacher-directed modeling. There are 17 words and four pictures. Read and discuss any unfamiliar words, then ask your students if they notice anything about the words (they all have an *a* in them). Ask about the vowel sounds in the middle of the words. Do they all have the same vowel sound? Students might cut their own sets of words in advance to bring to the group.

Demonstrate

Introduce the short -*a* symbol and the long -*a* symbol on the headers. Be sure to include the oddball header for words that do not fit the other two categories. Provide an example of each vowel sound and model the phoneme segmentation process involved in isolating and identifying each vowel sound. Demonstrate the sorting process by saying each word and comparing it to each key word, picture, and symbol. Have your students join in as you continue to model the isolation, identification, and categorization of the medial vowel sound. After sorting a few, be sure to model the word *what* and how to decide when a word does not fit either category. Explain why *what* is an oddball; *what* is spelled like it should have a short -*a* sound but it does not: The middle sound of *what* sounds like /uh/ instead of the short -*a* sound. When you are finished sorting, ask the students how the words in each column are alike and how they are different from the other words.

Sort

Have your students shuffle their cards and sort them into groups by short- and long-vowel sounds. Remember to have them head up their categories with the same key words and pictures that you used, including the oddball header. Tell your students to say each word aloud as they sort. The final sort should look like this (pictures are in brackets):

Short -a [cat]	Long -a [cake]	oddball
last	make	what
[glass]	face	
fast	same	
snap	[gate]	
sack	base	
ask	page	
grass	rake	
hand	came	
mad	[whale]	
[bat]	made	

Check

After the students sort, have them check their own sorts by reading each word and picture in a column to make sure they all sound the same in the middle. If a student does not notice a mistake, guide him or her to it by saying: *One of these doesn't fit. See if you can hear which one as I read them all.* Then read each word card, being careful to enunciate each vowel sound clearly. If the student still does not hear the oddball, read through the column again, then revisit the misplaced word and compare it to each key word and symbol. Ask the student which column the word should go in and why.

Reflect, Declare, and Compare

After checking the sort, ask your students to reflect on their sort and declare their categories by sound and by pattern. You might have students write how the words in one column are alike and how they are different from the words in the other.

Extend

Have students store their words and pictures in an envelope or plastic bag so they can reuse them throughout the week in individual and buddy sorts. Students should repeat this sort several times. Additional, similar sorts may be downloaded from *WTW* CD-ROM. See the list of standard weekly routines to form follow-up activities to the basic sorting lesson.

More Difficult Words: (16) *fact, sand, bath, math, tame, grape, flame, scale, fame, lane, whale, wade, blame, fake, blaze, skate.*

SORT 8   SHORT -*I* VERSUS LONG -*I* (CVCe)

Prepare a set of pictures and words to use for teacher-directed modeling as described in sort 7. There are 16 words and five pictures. Read and discuss any unfamiliar words. Ask your students what they notice about the spelling of the words in the sort.

Demonstrate

Introduce the short -*i* and the long -*i* symbols on the headers. Be sure to include the odd-ball header for words that do not fit the other two categories. Tell your students that they will compare and contrast the spelling patterns of short- and long -*i* words. Remember to segment the middle vowel sound in the key words so that students will know what to listen for. Demonstrate the sorting process by saying the word and comparing it to each key word, picture, and symbol. Have your students join in as you continue to model the isolation, identification, and categorization of the medial vowel sound. After you have sorted a few, hold up the word *give* and ask what pattern the word might go with. Then ask if the word *give* has a long -*i* sound. Explain that the word *give* is an oddball because it is spelled like a long -*i* word—it has the CVCe pattern—but the vowel sound in the middle of *give* is short. When you are finished demonstrating the sort, ask your students how the words in each column are alike and how they are different.

Sort

Have your students shuffle their cards and sort them into groups by short- and long-vowel sounds. Remember to have them head up their categories with the same vowel symbol, key words, and pictures that you used, including the oddball header. Have your students say each word aloud as they sort. The final sort should look like the one below. Key words are bolded and pictures are in brackets.

Short -*i* [pig]	Long -*i* [kite]	oddball
swim	**five**	give
rich	drive	
[stick]	mice	
thin	[dice]	
flip	hike	
gift	nice	
[clip]	life	
spill	[knife]	
[kick]	nine	
dish	prize	

Check

After the students sort, have them check their own sorts by reading each word and pic-ture in a column to make sure they all sound the same in the middle. If a student does not notice a mistake, guide him or her to it by saying: *One of these doesn't fit. See if you can hear which one as I read them all.* Then read each word card, being careful to enunciate each vowel sound clearly. Most students will notice their error when you do this, but if the student does not, read through the column again, then revisit the misplaced word and compare it to each key word and symbol.

Reflect, Declare, and Compare

After checking the sort, ask your students to reflect on their sort and declare their cate-gories by sound and by pattern. You might ask students to write what they learned about spelling short -*i* and long -*i* words from doing this sort in their word study note-books.

Extend

Have students store their words and pictures in an envelope or plastic bag so they can reuse them in individual and buddy sorts. Students should repeat this sort several times throughout the week. Use the standard weekly routines for follow-up activities to this basic sorting lesson; especially Writing Sorts, Change-O, Word Hunts, and Blind or No-Peeking Sorts.

More Difficult Words: (16) *slid, grin, skip, grip, shine, glide, pride, spine, tribe, ripe, pine, price, file, hive, smile, while.*

SORT 9   SHORT -*O* VERSUS LONG -*O* (CVCe)

There are 17 words and four pictures in this sort. Introduce this sort in a manner similar to that described for sorts 7 and 8. As you read and discuss the words, be sure to talk about the meanings of the words *rode* and *hole* so that students do not confuse them with the words *road* and *whole*. Explain that *rode* and *hole* are homophones—words that sound alike but have different meanings and different spelling patterns. The words *come* and *some* are oddballs in this sort because they have the CVCe spelling pattern but do not have the long -*o* sound. Conduct this sort using the same lesson format: **Demonstrate, sort, check, reflect,** and **extend.** The sort will end up looking something like this:

Short -*o* [sock]	Long -*o* [bone]	oddball
rock	**home**	come
job	stove	some
hot	hose	
spot	[cone]	
[pot]	hope	
chop	those	
[clock]	joke	
	rode*	
	broke	
	rose	
	hole*	
	[rope]	

*homophones

More Difficult Words: (16) *flock, plot, flop, slot, plop, lone, pole, woke, mole, tone, vote, robe, role, choke, stole, once.*

SORT 10   SHORT -*U* VERSUS LONG -*U* (CVCe)

This sort contains 16 words, five pictures, and three headers. Introduce the sort in a manner similar to sorts 7 and 8. The word *put* is an oddball because it has the short -*u* CVC pattern but it is pronounced as if it rhymes with *foot* instead of *cut*. Note: There is a slight difference in the long -*u* sound in *use* and *cute* (where the vowel says its name $y\overline{oo}$) and in *tune* and *flute* ($\overline{oo}$). Children may or may not notice this difference. Either way, the sound is spelled the same.

Demonstrate, sort, check, reflect, and **extend.** The sort will look something like this:

Short -*u* [cup]	Long -*u* [tube]	oddball
just	tube	put
drum	huge	
[bus]	June	
hunt	[cube]	
jump	rude	
shut	flute	
club	[mule]	
[cut]	cute	
such	tune	
[plus]	use	

More Difficult Words: (10) *crush, pump, plum, snug, plug, spun, plus, fuse, plume, prude.*

SORT 11   SHORT VERSUS LONG (CVC AND CVCe) REVIEW

There are 21 words in this sort and no pictures. Note that the column headers for this sort are different. The column headers label the pattern of consonants and vowels for each vowel sound. The label *CVC* refers to the consonant(s) to the left and right of the short vowel. The label *CVCe* refers to the pattern of consonants and vowels for the long vowel. Read and discuss any unfamiliar words. See if anyone knows which word is a homophone and tell your students that this *which* is spelled differently from the *witch* that rides a broomstick; they have different spelling patterns so we can tell them apart.

Demonstrate

Introduce headers *CVC-short, CVCe-long,* and *oddball*. Tell your students that they will be comparing and contrasting the short- and long-vowel spellings of all four of the vowels they have been studying in the previous four sorts. Since all four vowels are represented, the key words and pictures for individual vowels have been dropped. Explain that the CVC refers to the consonant-vowel-consonant spelling pattern of the short vowels. Write up several words and label them. *Fat* = CVC, but so is *flat* and *flock*. Label the consonants in *crop* as CCVC and in *which* as CCVCC. Explain that all three words have a short vowel and CVC is used to represent all of them. The CVCe refers to the consonant-vowel-consonant -*e* spelling pattern of the long vowels. Demonstrate the sorting process by saying each word and comparing it to each header. Have your students join you as you model sorting by pattern. See if they can spot the oddballs—the words *done* and *have* contain the CVCe pattern—but not the long-vowel sound. When you are finished demonstrating the sort, ask your students how the words in each column are alike by sound and by pattern. Reflect as a group on the pattern-to-sound consistency in the CVC and CVCe pattern across all four vowels.

Sort

Ask your students to sort independently and in buddy pairs.

Check

Since this sort does not include pictures, the ubiquitous silent -*e* at the end of so many words may tempt some students to sort by pattern alone. They may categorize all of the words with an *e* at the end into one group together. Without sorting by sound as well as pattern, however, the words *done* and *have* will no doubt be misplaced. If this is the case, ask your students to read all of the words in a column aloud to make sure they all have the same sound.

Reflect

Ask your students to reflect on the patterns characteristic of short- and long-vowel sounds in this review.

CVC-short	CVCe-long	oddball
crop	**note**	done
wax	mule	have
skin	rule	
crab	dune	
lots	safe	
gum	wife	
drip	cape	
which	tide	
	vote	
	wipe	
	race	

Extend

See the list of standard weekly routines. At this point you can also **review** all four long vowels using pictures and words from sorts 7, 8, 9, and 10. Challenge students to sort into four categories. You might try this with just the words by creating your own word sort sheet using the template at the back of this book. List long-vowel words from all four vowels randomly for students to cut apart and sort by long-vowel sounds. Follow this up with blind or no-peeking writing sorts where children take turns reading the words for their partner to write.

More Difficult Words: (16) *slap, shade, mate, chip, spite, slice, sob, owe, wove, stroke, mast, crate, clip, wide, phone, dove.*

SORT 12   FINAL /K/ SOUND SPELLED *CK*, *KE*, OR *K*

Students in the within word pattern stage may overgeneralize the final *ck* digraph in long-vowel words and spell the word *smoke*, SMOCKE, for example. Students need to discover that the final /k/ sound in single-syllable words is directly related to the vowel sound that precedes it. These spelling distinctions are tied directly to the vowel sound.

There are 21 words in this sort. Prepare a set of words and headers to use for teacher-directed modeling. Note that the column headers for this sort are different—they reflect the spelling of the final /k/ sound in three different vowel-sound contrasts. Read and discuss any unfamiliar words. Ask your students if there is anything they notice about all of the words (they all have *k* in them). You may want to cut off the headers and ask students to do an open sort. Some may sort by pattern, others by sound. Either way the results will be similar.

Demonstrate

Introduce headers *ck*, *ke*, and *k*. Tell your students that they will be comparing and contrasting the spelling of the final /k/ sound. Demonstrate the sorting process by using the bolded key words: *kick*, and *take*, and *took*. Say each word and compare it to each header. Have your students join you as you continue to model sorting by the spelling of the final /k/ sound at the end of each word. When you are finished demonstrating the sort, ask your students how the words in each column are alike by vowel sound. See if they notice that all of the words ending in *ck* have short-vowel sounds; all of the words ending in *ke* have long-vowel sounds; and all of the words ending in *k* have vowel sounds that are neither long nor short. If your students do not notice this on their own, read the words in each column carefully and tell them directly. At this point you might compare the *ck* spelling to the CVC pattern of previous sorts and point out that it is still a CVC pattern. Likewise, compare the *ke* spelling to the CVCe pattern of the previous sort. Read all of the words in the *k* column aloud and ask the students what they notice about them (they rhyme and they all have the same spelling pattern).

After your demonstration, have the students **sort, check,** and then **reflect** on this sort. Be sure to have them **declare** what spellings go with which vowel sounds. The sort will look something like this:

-ck short	-ke long	-k other
kick	take	took
sick	bike	shook
lock	shake	cook
duck	spoke	look
pack	duke	book
lick	strike	
sock	smoke	
truck	like	

Extend

See the list of standard weekly routines: Writing Sorts, Change-O, Word Hunts, No-Peeking Sorts, and Games. You might try dictating a sentence like: *Take a snack in your pack when you go for a hike.* See also the Take-A-Card game on the *WTW* CD-ROM for more *ck, ke,* and *k* spellings.

More Difficult Words: (14) *stack, track, quack, brake, quake, flake, wake, brick, chick, click, spike, poke, clove, pluck.*

SPELL CHECK 1
ASSESSMENT FOR SHORT- AND LONG (CVCe)-VOWEL PATTERNS

The spelling of short vowels following the consonant-vowel-consonant (CVC) pattern and the spelling of long vowels following the consonant-vowel-consonant-silent *-e* patterns (CVCe) are assessed with the Spell Check for Short and Long (CVCe) on page 28. All of the words pictured have been presented previously in sorts 7–12. Name each picture, then ask your students to think about each word's vowel sound and write the spelling of the word on the lines provided. Students can also complete this independently. These are the 20 words assessed:

1. hose	2. tube	3. duck
4. tape	5. book	6. sack
7. bone	8. kick	9. sock
10. mule	11. bike	12. flute
13. five	14. rock	15. smoke
16. stove	17. rake	18. kite
19. lock	20. cape	

SORT 7   Short -*a* versus Long -*a* (CVCe)

ǎ 🐱 cat	ā 🍰 cake	*oddball*
mad		make
fast	hand	what
	snap	last
page	came	
	grass	face
base	rake	ask
same	made	sack

SORT 8   Short -*i* versus Long -*i* (CVCe)

ĭ 🐷 pig	ī ◇ kite	*oddball*
dish		five
rich	mice	prize
	gift	hike
life	flip	
	thin	swim
nice	drive	spill
nine	give	

ŏ sock	ō bone	*oddball*
rock		rode
job	hope	those
	hot	hose
joke	home	
	come	hole
some	spot	chop
stove	rose	broke

SORT 10   Short -u versus Long -u (CVCe)

ŭ cup	ū tube	*oddball*
drum		cute
use	huge	just
	jump	hunt
shut	tube	
2 + 2 = 4	tune	such
club	June	rude
flute		put

CVC - short	CVCe - long	*oddball*
crop	note	mule
done	wax	rule
dune	skin	safe
crab	wife	lots
cape	tide	gum
have	drip	vote
race	which	wipe

-ck short	-ke long	-k other
kick	**take**	**took**
bike	sick	lock
shook	shake	duck
duke	spoke	pack
strike	cook	lick
sock	smoke	look
truck	like	book

1. _____
_ _ _ _ _ _ _ _ _ _ _
_____

2. _____
_ _ _ _ _ _ _ _ _ _ _
_____

3. _____
_ _ _ _ _ _ _ _ _ _ _
_____

4. _____
_ _ _ _ _ _ _ _ _ _ _
_____

5. _____
_ _ _ _ _ _ _ _ _ _ _
_____

6. _____
_ _ _ _ _ _ _ _ _ _ _
_____

7. _____
_ _ _ _ _ _ _ _ _ _ _
_____

8. _____
_ _ _ _ _ _ _ _ _ _ _
_____

9. _____
_ _ _ _ _ _ _ _ _ _ _
_____

10. _____
_ _ _ _ _ _ _ _ _ _ _
_____

11. _____
_ _ _ _ _ _ _ _ _ _ _
_____

12. _____
_ _ _ _ _ _ _ _ _ _ _
_____

13. _____
_ _ _ _ _ _ _ _ _ _ _
_____

14. _____
_ _ _ _ _ _ _ _ _ _ _
_____

15. _____
_ _ _ _ _ _ _ _ _ _ _
_____

16. _____
_ _ _ _ _ _ _ _ _ _ _
_____

17. _____
_ _ _ _ _ _ _ _ _ _ _
_____

18. _____
_ _ _ _ _ _ _ _ _ _ _
_____

19. _____
_ _ _ _ _ _ _ _ _ _ _
_____

20. _____
_ _ _ _ _ _ _ _ _ _ _
_____

SORTS 13-18

Common Long-Vowel Patterns (CVCe and CVVC)

NOTES FOR THE TEACHER

Another common long-vowel pattern is the consonant-vowel-vowel-consonant (CVVC) pattern. Every vowel except the vowel *i* uses this pattern to represent the long-vowel sound. In these six sorts we present the most common CVVC patterns for the vowels *a*, *o*, *u*, and *e*. Although the CVVC pattern is the new long-vowel spelling pattern introduced in this section, previously studied vowel sounds and patterns, including the CVCe of the previous six sorts, reappear in new words and provide a starting point for comparison. Since the vowel *i* does not use the CVVC pattern, other vowel patterns for *i* are presented in the next section.

Sorts 13–18 are designed for early-to-middle within word pattern stage spellers who are using but confusing the CVVC and CVCe patterns. They might spell the word *foam*, FOME; or the word *slope*, SLOAP. Most of the words in these sorts are on a second- and third-grade level, though harder words are listed at the end of each lesson for students with a more advanced reading vocabulary. You might use the Spell Check on page 43 as a pretest to see which of your students are in need of these sorts. Students who spell most of the words on the Spell Check correctly may benefit from the study of less common long-vowel patterns, such as the ones presented in sorts 19–24. Different pacing schemes for the within word pattern stage are suggested in *WTW*.

Each of these six sorts contains 19 to 21 words plus three to four column headers. **Key words** have been bolded on the sort sheet and these should be placed at the top of each column. Key words are the most frequently occurring words of that particular spelling pattern. **Oddballs** are high-frequency words whose pattern violates the dominant pattern-to-sound correspondence. For example, the word *said* is an oddball because it does not contain the long -*a* sound even though it has the CVVC pattern associated with the long -*a* sound. See Chapter 6 of *WTW* for more information about teaching high-frequency words.

The sequence of long-vowel sorts could easily be done in a different order. The patterns for *e* are presented last because a common CVVC pattern for long -*e* overlaps with a similar pattern for the short -*e* sound. Sort 18 reviews the CVVC pattern across vowels.

Most children need more than one week to learn all the common long-vowel patterns for each of the vowels, but the recursive nature of word study makes it possible to generalize the most common patterns across vowels. Such is the goal of sorts 13–18 that address the CVVC pattern in four long vowels. If your students seem to be catching on to the CVVC pattern quickly, speed up your pace. A slower pace is suggested in *WTW* and additional words and sorts may be found in the *WTW* Appendix. Whatever pace your students need, be sure to provide ample opportunities to sort first by sound, and then by pattern. Ultimately you want your students to be able to categorize words by sound and pattern simultaneously.

When possible, share books that contain a number of words with the targeted spelling feature. For example, *Frog and Toad Together* (Lobel, 1971) is a natural connection with the short- and long-vowel sounds for *o* and contains many examples of the CVCe and CVVC patterns.

STANDARD WEEKLY ROUTINES FOR USE WITH SORTS 13–18

1. **Repeated Work with Word Sorts:** Students should work with the word sorts several times after the sort has been modeled and discussed, as described in each lesson below.
2. **Writing Sorts and Word Study Notebooks:** Students should record their word sorts by writing them into columns in their word study notebooks, as described before. It is a good idea to have students write their reflections about what they learned about the spelling of these words in their word study notebooks after they have recorded their sort.
3. **Word-O:** Ask students to conduct a word operation (Word-O) on 5 to 10 words. Add, subtract, or substitute consonants to make a new word. Start with the word *space,* for example, and subtract the *s* to get *pace.* Add an *l* to *pace* to get *place.* Subtract the *p* to get *lace.* Substitute an *n* for the *c* and get *lane.* Students can record their word operations in their word study notebooks by writing the new word to the right of the original word. You might ask them to underline the letters that were changed in their operation.
4. **Word Hunts:** A word hunt is a search for additional exemplars of a pattern being studied. Be sure students use previously read text so that their comprehension of the material has already occurred and they can skim through the words quickly and easily. Direct students to texts that you know contain the pattern or limit the amount of time that students are hunting. Students should record the words they find in the proper column in their word study notebook and share them with the group when they meet.
5. **Dictated Sentences:** Prepare a sentence that contains several of your word study words, read it to your students, and have them write it. Provide feedback about spelling and mechanics.
6. **Blind or No-Peeking Sorts and No-Peeking Writing Sorts:** After students sort their words several times have them test their memory for pattern-to-sound consistencies with blind or *no-peeking sorts,* and blind or *no-peeking writing sorts.* One student calls out a word without showing it; the other student points to the column in which it belongs. Or, the second partner writes the word under a key word. In either case the word card is shown later and students check the spelling.
7. **Homework:** See the homework form in the Appendix.
8. **Games and Other Activities:** Create games and activities such as those in *WTW* or download them ready made from the *WTW* CD-ROM. The Race Track game is one we highly recommend for use with long-vowel patterns. There are other games described in Chapter 6 of *WTW.*
9. **Assessment:** To assess students' weekly mastery, ask them to spell the words. An assessment of the long-vowel CVVC pattern used in these sorts follows on page 43: Spell Check 2: CVVC Patterns.

SORT 13 SHORT -A AND LONG -A (CVCe AND CVVC)

Demonstrate

This sort has 20 words, including two oddballs and four headers. Prepare the words to use for teacher-directed modeling. You will also need a short -a symbol and a long -a symbol from the symbol template in the back of the book.

Read and discuss the meanings of any unfamiliar words. Be sure to point out the homophone *main* and discuss its meaning. Tell your students that the other *mane*, the hair on a lion or a horse's head, is spelled with a different spelling pattern because it has a different meaning. Ask if anyone sees any other homophones in the set (*tail; pain*). Ask your students what they notice about the spelling of these words. Proceed to demonstrate this two-step sort: (1) sort by sound; then, (2) sort by pattern.

Sort by Sound

Display a short -a symbol, a long -a symbol from the Appendix, and the word *oddball* at the top of three separate columns. Do not use the pattern headers (*CVC, CVCe, CVVC*) yet. Tell your students that the short -a symbol stands for the short -a sound in the middle of such words as *Jack*. Segment the middle vowel sound so they know where to focus their attention (e.g., /J/ /a/ /k/). Next, explain that the long -a symbol stands for the long -a sound in the middle of words such as *space* or *rain* where you can hear the letter *a* say its name. Again, segment the middle vowel sound to make the long -a sound and location explicit. Finally, begin the **sound sort.** Model the placement of a key word, segment the middle vowel, and explain what you are doing: *Here is the word, Jack. Jack has a short -a sound in the middle so I will put it under the short -a symbol. This is the word <u>space</u>. <u>Space</u> has a long -a sound in the middle so I will put it under the long -a symbol. Here is the word <u>rain.</u> R-ai-n. <u>Rain</u> has a long -a sound in the middle so I will put it under the long -a symbol with <u>space</u>. Now who can help me sort the rest of these words?* Continue on in this vein having the students help you sort all the words by sound. When all the words have been sorted, read them in columns and check for any that need to be changed: *Do all of these words sound alike in the middle? Do we need to move any?*

NOTE: Some of your students may have trouble with the word *camp*. The nasal sound made by the letter *m* makes it difficult to segment the medial vowel sound apart from the nasal. Tell your students to pronounce the word without the nasal (*cap*) to see if they can hear the vowel sound that way. At this time, it is also likely that you may want to move the words *said* and *want* into the oddball category. Since neither of these words has a short or long -a vowel sound, they do not belong in either column.

Sort by Pattern

Ask your students what they notice about the words in the long -a column. *Could we put any of those words together?* Next, display the CVCe and CVVC as pattern headers under the long -a symbol. See if your students can find all of the words in the long -a column that are spelled with one of these two patterns: the consonant-vowel-consonant-silent -e pattern (CVCe), or the consonant-vowel-vowel-consonant pattern (CVVC). Proceed to model a **pattern sort** for the long -a word. Ask your students why *said* is an oddball. Help them understand that even though *said* is spelled with the CVVC pattern, it does not have a long -a sound in the middle.

Sort by Sound and Pattern

Add the consonant-vowel-consonant (CVC) pattern header for the short-vowel column and mix up all of your words. Repeat the sort, categorizing this time by vowel sound and by long-vowel patterns at the same time. **Check** the sort, then **reflect** about how the words in each column are alike. The sort will end up looking like this:

CVC	CVCe	CVVC	oddball
Jack	**space**	**rain**	said
black	frame	brain	want
flash	place	paint	
rash	blame	train	
camp		main	
		faint	
		pain	
		chain	
		tail	

Sort, Check, Reflect, and Extend

Give each student a copy of the sort and assign the task of cutting out the words and sorting them individually. On subsequent days students should repeat the sort several times. Use the standard weekly routines (Writing Sorts, Word Operations, Word Hunts, Blind or No-Peeking Sorts, etc.) for follow-up activities to this basic sorting lesson.

Suggested Words for Word Operations: *space, frame, brain, train, camp.*

More Difficult Words: (11) *gasp, lamp, smash, stamp, crash, trace, paste, waste, waist, bait, claim.*

SORT 14   SHORT –*O* AND LONG -*O* (CVCe AND CVVC)

Demonstrate

This sort contains 21 words and three headers. The *oddball* column header has been dropped because we want students to look for "the odd ones out" on their own now. Sort first by sound, so *drove* and *road* will be in the same column. Read and discuss the meaning of the words and be sure to note the homophone *whole* and its partner with a different meaning, *hole,* in sort 9. The word *knock* is worth a second look to discuss the silent *k* at the beginning. Introduce the sort in a manner similar to sort 13. First, sort by sound using the short -*o* and long -*o* headers from the Appendix on page 134; then, sort by pattern using the pattern headers on the sort. You could also begin the lesson with an open sort by cutting off the headers before duplicating the sort. Ask your students to cut apart your words and see if they can discover the categories for themselves before they come to the group sort under your direction. You might ask students if they can brainstorm other words that rhyme with the oddball *love (dove, shove).*

CVC	CVCe	CVVC	
lost	**drove**	**road***	love
knock	stone	float	none
soft	chose	boat	
cross	slope	goat	
	whole*	soap	
		foam	
		load	
		toast	
		toad	
		coat	

*homophone

Sort, Check, Reflect, and Extend

Give each student a copy of the sort and assign the task of cutting out the words and sorting them individually in the same way they did in the group. On subsequent days, students should repeat the sorting activity several times and complete the standard weekly routines in their word study notebook: Writing Sorts, Word Operations, Word Hunts, Blind or No-Peeking Sorts, and so on.

Suggested Words for Word-O: *whole, chose, toad, boat, foam, cross.*

More Difficult Words: (9) *shop, drop, cove, doze, oak, croak, groan, moat, goal.*

SORT 15   SHORT –*U* AND LONG -*U* (CVCe AND CVVC)

Demonstrate, Sort, Check, and Reflect

This sort contains 20 words and four headers. The sort is somewhat different from previous sorts because the most frequent CVVC pattern for the long -*u* sound is spelled *oo*. While the *ui* pattern is quite limited (there are really only three high-frequency long -*u* words spelled with the *ui* pattern), we include it here with *Common Long-Vowel Patterns* since it is also a CVVC pattern. The oddballs in this sort, *build* and *built*, also contain the *ui* pattern but not the long -*u* sound. No oddball header is provided, however, since students should be accustomed to finding "the odd ones out" by now and putting them to the side when they sort. Key words have been bolded and should be placed at the top under each header. Read and discuss the meaning of the words, then introduce the sort in a manner similar to sorts 13 and 14. First, sort by sound; then, sort by pattern.

CVC	CVCe	CVVC	CVVC	
crust	**cube**	**food**	**fruit**	build
bump	dude	bloom	suit	built
skunk	prune	smooth	juice	
trust		broom		
		mood		
		moon		
		spoon		
		tooth		

Extend

Have students complete the standard weekly routines in their word study notebook: Writing Sorts, Word Operations, Word Hunts, Blind or No-Peeking Sorts, and so on.

Suggested Words for Word Operations: *bump, dude, bloom, spoon, food.*

More Difficult Words: (14) *rust, fuss, dusk, blush, gust, crude, mute, fume, loop, scoop, loom, booth, cruise, bruise.*

SORT 16   SHORT –*E* AND LONG -*E* (CVVC)

Demonstrate, Sort, Check, and Reflect

This sort contains 21 words, three headers, and the oddball *been*. Like sort 15, this sort includes two CVVC patterns for the long -*e* sound: *ee* and *ea*. Conveniently, the homophones *week* and *weak* are included to call attention to the fact that words with different meanings must have different spellings to tell them apart when we read and spell. Read and discuss the meaning of the words, then introduce the sort in a manner similar to sorts 13, 14, and 15. First, sort by sound; then, sort by pattern. *Been* is an oddball.

CVC	CVVC-ee	CVVC-ea	
less	**feet**	**mean**	been
web	keep	heat	
next	green	team	
	sleep	speak	
	sweep	clean	
	teeth	weak*	
	jeep	leaf	
	week*	teach	
		peach	

*homophones

Extend

Have students complete the standard weekly routines in their word study notebook: Writing Sorts, Word Operations, Word Hunts, Blind or No-Peeking Writing Sorts, and so on.

Suggested Words for Word Operations: *next, sleep, heat, weak, teach.*

More Difficult Words: (11) *stem, pest, speech, speed, greed, creep, creek, least, deal, meal, treat.*

SORT 17   "THE DEVIL SORT" SHORT -*E* (CVC AND CVVC) AND LONG -*E* (CVVC)

Demonstrate, Sort, Check, and Reflect

Sort 17 contains 20 words and four headers. This sort is hard because it includes two CVVC patterns for the long -*e* sound (*ee* and *ea*) and two patterns for the short-*e* sound: CVC and CVVC. It is called "The Devil Sort" because the *ea* pattern is used to spell both the short-*e* and the long -*e* sound. Fortunately, many of the short -*e ea* words rhyme, so if you show this to your students they will be able to remember them as a group: *dead, head,* and *bread* all rhyme and they all end in *ead*.

Be sure to read and discuss the meaning of the words, especially the pronunciation and meaning of the word *lead*. The word *lead* is a homograph and can be pronounced with either a short or long -*e* sound, so it may be sorted in either sound category. Discuss the shift in meaning that accompanies the shift in the vowel sound. The homophone *when* can provide an opportunity to review the short -*e* sound and contrast it with the short -*i* sound in its homophone partner, *win*. The oddball *great* is a high-frequency word that contains the *ea* pattern but has a long -*a* sound instead of a long -*e* sound. Discussing these will enrich your students' word knowledge.

After discussing the words, introduce the sort in a manner similar to the previous four sorts. Use the long -*e* and short -*e* headers from the Appendix to sort first by sound, then use the pattern headers on the sort to sort by the patterns of CVC and CVVC. You will need to introduce the CVVC pattern header for the short-vowel sound category before you model the pattern sort. Remind your students that they have sorted the CVVC pattern before and it was always associated with the long-vowel sound. Now, they will learn some short -*e* words that have the same pattern.

Short -*e* CVC	Short -*e* CVVC	Long -*e* CVVC-*ee*	Long -*e* CVVC-*ea*	
when*	dead	trees	each	great
sled	head	street	reach	
	bread	queen	seat	
	breath	sweet	dream	
	death		lead*	
			steam	
			beach	
			east	

*homophone or homograph

Extend

After students have repeated this sort many times, have them complete the standard weekly routines in their word study notebook: Writing Sorts, Word Operations, Word Hunts, Blind or No-Peeking Writing Sorts, and so on.

Suggested Words for Word Operations: *bread, street, reach, steam, east.*

More Difficult Words: (15) *swept, shelf, wealth, breast, health, tread, beef, geese, breeze, peel, greet, flea, peak, leak, leash.*

SORT 18   REVIEW FOR CVVC PATTERN (AI-OA-EE-EA)
Demonstrate, Sort, Check, and Reflect

This is a review sort for the CVVC patterns for the vowels *a, o,* and *e*. The CVVC patterns for *u* are not included in this review because the *oo* pattern for the long -*u* sound is quite memorable by virtue of the double *os,* and the *ui* pattern has few exemplars. If you wish to include the *oo* and *ui* patterns for the long -*u* sound in this CVVC review, simply recycle the long -*u* word cards from sort 15 and add them in. Otherwise, these are 24 new words that contain the familiar CVVC pattern and all but four represent the long-vowel sound. The four short vowels contain the *ea* pattern for the short -*e*. Headers are not included here because you will want your students to sort by sound and by pattern on their own after your demonstration. Alternatively, you can challenge your students to do an open sort and determine their own categories. At this point, an open sort will give you diagnostic information about how the students are thinking about pattern-to-sound consistencies.

First read and discuss these new words, calling special attention to the meaning of the homophone *mail.* Ask if anyone knows the meaning and spelling of the other *male.* See if anyone can spot the other homophone in the sort (*sail*) and predict how its partner would be spelled (*sale*). The homograph *read* is also worthy of discussion since the verb tense changes depending on whether you pronounce it with a short or long -*e* sound. This word may be sorted with the *ea* pattern for either the short -*e* group or the long -*e* group, depending on pronunciation. Remind students of a similar phenomenon with the word *lead* in the previous sort. Many students are likely to be unfamiliar with the word *dread,* so be sure to use this word in a meaningful sentence and talk about its meaning.

After your discussion, demonstrate how to sort these words by vowel sound (long -*a*, long -*e*, long -*o*, and short -*e*). Then sort the long -*e* group into two columns by pattern. Mix up the words and then model sorting by sound and pattern simultaneously. It is helpful if you "think aloud" as you sort and model your mental processes. The sort will look something like this:

wait	thread	need	beast	toast
mail*	read*	sheep	seat	coast
sail*	deaf	wheel	neat	moan
rail	meant	three	pea	throat
	dread	sheets	cream	
		cheek		

*homophones or homographs

Extend

After students have repeated this sort many times, have them complete the standard weekly routines in their word study notebook: Writing Sorts, Word Operations, Word Hunts, Blind or No-Peeking Writing Sorts, and so on. Additional vowel pattern sorts for *e* may be downloaded from the *WTW* CD-ROM.

Suggested Words for Word Operations: *wheel, cream, pea, moan, rail.*

NOTE: *Word Operations on these words are likely to result in the creation of other homophones whose meanings bear discussion (substitute* st *for the* wh *of* wheel *and get* steel).

SPELL CHECK 2
ASSESSING THE CVVC LONG-VOWEL PATTERN
FOR A, E, O, AND U

The spelling of long vowels following the consonant-vowel-vowel-consonant (CVVC) pattern is assessed with the Spell Check for CVVC on page 43. All of the words pictured have been presented previously in sorts 13–18. Name each picture, and then ask your students to write the spelling of the word on the lines provided. Students can also complete this independently. These are the words assessed:

1. leaf	2. suit	3. beach
4. rain	5. toast	6. teeth
7. chain	8. peach	9. road
10. feet	11. mail	12. queen
13. pea	14. toad	15. fruit
16. broom	17. sail	18. soap
19. spoon	20. coat	

ă CVC	ā CVCe	ā CVVC
oddball	**space**	**rain**
Jack	black	pain
brain	paint	place
rash	blame	train
main	faint	want
chain	camp	tail
said	frame	flash

ŏ CVC	ō CVCe	ō CVVC
lost	**drove**	**road**
chose	boat	love
goat	soap	knock
slope	foam	load
whole	none	toast
soft	toad	coat
float	cross	stone

SORT 15   Short -*u* and Long -*u* (CVCe and CVVC)

$\breve{u}$ CVC	$\bar{u}$ CVCe	$\bar{u}$i CVVC
$\overline{oo}$ CVVC	cube	food
fruit	crust	bloom
smooth	suit	built
dude	skunk	broom
mood	bump	juice
trust	build	moon
prune	spoon	tooth

ĕ CVC	ēe CVVC	ēa CVVC
less	**feet**	**mean**
green	team	been
sleep	web	speak
clean	keep	sweep
teeth	heat	week
weak	next	peach
leaf	teach	jeep

SORT 17 "The Devil Sort" Short -e and Long -e (CVC and CVVC)

ĕ CVC	e̅a CVVC	e̅e CVVC
ĕa CVVC	when	dead
trees	each	reach
head	queen	east
street	bread	seat
dream	great	lead
steam	sled	sweet
breath	beach	death

wait	read	need
beast	toast	wheel
sheep	seat	coast
mail	deaf	three
neat	moan	sheets
meant	rail	cheek
pea	throat	dread
cream	sail	thread

Words Their Way: Word Sorts for Within Word Pattern Spellers © 2004 by Prentice-Hall, Inc.

Spell Check 2 Sorts 13-18 CVVC Patterns   Name _____

1. _____ _ _ _ _ _ _ _ _ _ _____	2. _____ _ _ _ _ _ _ _ _ _ _____
3. _____ _ _ _ _ _ _ _ _ _ _____	4. _____ _ _ _ _ _ _ _ _ _ _____
5. _____ _ _ _ _ _ _ _ _ _ _____	6. _____ _ _ _ _ _ _ _ _ _ _____
7. _____ _ _ _ _ _ _ _ _ _ _____	8. _____ _ _ _ _ _ _ _ _ _ _____
9. _____ _ _ _ _ _ _ _ _ _ _____	10. _____ _ _ _ _ _ _ _ _ _ _____
11. _____ _ _ _ _ _ _ _ _ _ _____	12. _____ _ _ _ _ _ _ _ _ _ _____
13. _____ _ _ _ _ _ _ _ _ _ _____	14. _____ _ _ _ _ _ _ _ _ _ _____
15. _____ _ _ _ _ _ _ _ _ _ _____	16. _____ _ _ _ _ _ _ _ _ _ _____
17. _____ _ _ _ _ _ _ _ _ _ _____	18. _____ _ _ _ _ _ _ _ _ _ _____
19. _____ _ _ _ _ _ _ _ _ _ _____	20. _____ _ _ _ _ _ _ _ _ _ _____

Less Common Long-Vowel Patterns

NOTES FOR THE TEACHER

Sorts 19–24 present a variety of other long-vowel patterns. We examine the less common vowel patterns for the vowels *a, o, u,* and *i* in a series of six sorts. The long-vowel patterns introduced in these sorts are less common because they occur in harder words. Also, some patterns end in a vowel sound (e.g., *lay, chew, cry*) and thus introduce the *open syllable* concept. (An open syllable ends in a vowel sound as opposed to being "closed" with a consonant that you can hear.) Other less common long-vowel patterns introduced in this section include the CVCC patterns in words such as *told, mild,* or *light.* As you can probably tell, we increased the cognitive load in these sorts by including more words, harder words, words that address a new concept (the open syllable), and, for some vowels, a new pattern. Although the open syllable and the CVCC patterns are the new spelling features introduced in this section, previously studied vowel sounds and patterns, including the CVCe and CVCC patterns from earlier sorts, reappear in new words and provide a starting point for comparison.

Sorts 19–24 are designed for middle within word pattern stage spellers who are using but confusing the less common long-vowel patterns. They might spell the word *told,* TOALD; or the word *mild,* MILED. Most of the words in these sorts are on a third- to fourth-grade level. Where possible, more difficult words are listed at the end of each lesson. You might use the Spell Check on page 58 as a pretest to see which of your students are in need of these sorts. Students who spell most of the words on the Spell Check correctly may benefit from the study of *r*-influenced vowels or diphthongs introduced in sorts 25–35 instead.

Each of these six sorts contains 23 to 24 words plus four column headers. Key words have been bolded and these should be placed at the top of each column. As always, key words are the most frequently occurring words of that particular spelling pattern. **Oddballs** are either high-frequency words whose patterns violate the dominant pattern-to-sound correspondence or are words that encompass features of two or more categories. For example, the word *lost* is an oddball because it does not contain the long -*o* sound of other CVCC words like *most* or *post,* but is consistent with short -*o* words with a similar pattern (e.g., *cost*).

This sequence of sorts could easily be done in a different order. The patterns for *o* are presented last since the CVCC pattern for long -*o* overlaps with a similar pattern for the short -*o* sound. Sort 24 reviews all of the long-vowel patterns studied up to this point.

While sorts 19–24 are decidedly more difficult than the previous 18 sorts, the recursive nature of word study makes it possible to generalize the new patterns introduced here across the vowels. This is the objective of sort 24 that reviews the CVCC, CVVC, and open-syllable patterns across all four vowels.

By this time your students should be adept at sorting by sound and by pattern. Since the focus of these sorts is on less common vowel patterns, and since only a few short-vowel words are included in each sort, you might be able to speed up the introductory process of sorting by sound first before sorting by pattern and try sorting by sound and pattern simultaneously. If students are experienced sorters, you may come to rely more on open sorts in which they are asked to cut apart their words and sort them into categories of sound and pattern before they come to the group lesson. Asking capable students to do these open sorts while you are working directly with another group can make managing several groups easier. Open sorts are also diagnostic and allow you to see what students are noticing about the orthography. You may want to cut off the headers before duplicating the words for open sorts. Also, remember to enlarge the sorts when copying to increase the size.

When possible, share books and poems that contain some words that are spelled with the targeted feature. For example, *Stellaluna* (by Janell Cannon) contains many examples of the VCC and open-syllable long-vowel patterns.

STANDARD WEEKLY ROUTINES FOR USE WITH SORTS 19–24

1. **Repeated Work with Word Sorts:** Students sort their own word cards independently and with partners throughout the week.
2. **Writing Sorts and Word Study Notebooks:** Students record their word sorts into columns in their notebooks and write reflections. It is a good idea to have students write about what they learned about the spelling of these words after they have recorded their sort.
3. **Speed Sorts:** Using a stopwatch, students time themselves as they sort their words into categories. After obtaining a baseline speed, students repeat the sort several times and try to beat their own time. Repeated, timed speed sorts help students internalize spelling patterns and become automatic in recognizing them.
4. **Word Hunts:** Students look for words in previously read material that are spelled with the same pattern under study, then add them to their word study notebook.
5. **Dictated Sentences:** Compose a sentence containing some word study words and have your students write it to your dictation. Provide feedback about spelling and mechanics.
6. **Blind or No-Peeking Sorts and No-Peeking Writing Sorts:** One student calls out a word without showing it; the other student points to the column it should go in. Or, the second partner writes the word under a key word. In either case, the word card is shown later and students check the spelling.
7. **Homework:** Additional sorts and writing sorts may be assigned for homework. See the homework form in the Appendix.
8. **Games and Other Activities:** Create games and activities such as those in *WTW* or download them ready made from the *WTW* CD-ROM.
9. **Assessment:** Students should be assessed weekly on each set of words. An assessment of all long-vowel CVVC patterns used in these sorts follows on page 58: *Spell Check 3: Less Common Long-Vowel Patterns.*

SORT 19   SHORT -*A* AND LONG -*A* (CVCe, CVVC-*AI*, AND OPEN SYLLABLE *AY*)

This sort contains 23 words and four headers. Begin as usual by reading and discussing the meaning of the words. Then, ask students what they notice about the spelling of the words. Next, display the short -*a* and long -*a* symbols with the pattern labels to head each of the four columns. Tell your students that they will learn a new pattern for the long -*a* sound in this sort: the *ay* pattern.

Demonstrate

Demonstrate the sort as in previous sorts. The word *raise* merits some discussion because it has the CVVC pattern *ai* in addition to an *e* at the end. Explain that the *e* at the end of *raise* is not the same kind of silent -*e* that makes the medial vowel "say its name" as in the CVCe pattern they have previously sorted. The *e* at the end of *raise* tells us that the final *s* is pronounced like a /z/ instead of an /s/. The word *raise* may or may not be considered an oddball. (Sort 40 explores *ce*, *ve*, and *se* endings.)

CVC	CVCe	CVVC-*ai*	CVV-*ay*
glass	**trade**	**Spain**	**lay**
stand	brave	grain	stay
past	slave	aid	play
	shape	nail	clay
	taste	gain	tray
		raise*	stray
			gray
			pray
			hay

*discuss final *e*

Help your students reflect on this sort. See if they notice that all of the *ay* words end in a long-vowel sound. Tell your students that a syllable or a one-syllable word that ends in a long-vowel sound is called an open syllable. One way of labeling an open-syllable pattern is to label it a CV or CVV pattern, since the *y* acts as a vowel in these long -*a* words.

Have your students **sort, check, reflect,** and **extend** this sort by completing the recommended standard weekly routines for sorts 19–24: Repeated Word Sorts, Writing Sorts, Speed Sorts, Word Hunts, Dictated Sentences, and Blind or No-Peeking Sorts.

More Difficult Words: (18) *grand, brass, task, tramp, grave, graze, lame, rate, slate, stale, faith, stain, fail, praise, jay, sway, ray, slay.*

SORT 20   SHORT -*O* AND LONG -*O* (CVCe, CVVC-*OA*, AND OPEN SYLLABLE *OW*)

Introduce the sort in a manner similar to sort 19 or you might want to try an open sort in which the students sort on their own before any discussion. As you read and discuss the words, be sure to call attention to the homophone pair *Rome* and *roam.* Also point out the word *know* and discuss the silent *k* at the beginning of that word. Remind them of the work *knock* from sort 14. See if they can spot another word that has a silent letter at the beginning (*wrote*). Tell your students that they will learn a new pattern for the long -*o* sound: the *ow* pattern.

Demonstrate

Demonstrate this sort as in previous sorts. The word *lose* will require some discussion because it has the CVCe pattern but does not contain the long -*o* sound. The word *lose* could be considered an oddball.

CVC	CVCe	CVVC-*oa*	CVV-*ow*	
stock	**froze**	**coal**	**show**	lose
long	globe	coach	blow	
	Rome*	roast	slow	
	close	oat	grow	
	wrote	loaf	flow	
		roam*	throw	
			row	
			mow	
			know	

*homophones

Help your students reflect on this sort. See what they think about the *ow* pattern in relation to the *open syllable* discussion in the previous sort. Remind them that when a syllable or a one-syllable word ends with a long-vowel sound, it is called an *open syllable*. One way of labeling the open-syllable pattern is by labeling it in a CV or CVV pattern since *w* acts like a vowel, not a consonant.

Have your students **sort, check, reflect,** and **extend** this sort by completing the recommended standard weekly routines for sorts 19–24: Repeated Word Sorts, Writing Sorts, Speed Sorts, Word Hunts, and Blind or No-Peeking Sorts. You might dictate the sentence: *Show the coach how you throw a slow ball close to the corner of home plate.*

More Difficult Words: (18) *dock, prompt, stomp, blond, sole, dome, pose, quote, rove, yoke, lope, zone, cloak, loaves, boast, coax, loan, broad.*

SORT 21   SHORT -*U* AND LONG -*U* (OPEN SYLLABLE *EW* AND *UE*)

Introduce the sort in a manner similar to the previous two sorts. As you read and discuss the words, be sure to discuss the meanings of the homophone pairs *dew* and *due, flew* and *flue, blew* and *blue.* Remind students that when words sound the same but have a different meaning, the words have a different spelling pattern so we can tell them apart. Ask if anyone can tell which two spelling patterns are alternated in these homophone pairs (*ew* and *ue*). Tell your students that *ew* and *ue* are the new spelling patterns they will learn for the long -*u* sound. Explain that the final *w* in the *ew* pattern acts like a vowel so that *dew, blew, flew,* and so on end in a vowel sound, just like the long -*o* words that ended in *ow* did. You might ask if anyone sees any other homophones in the long -*u* list and talk about the silent *k* in the word *knew* and how *knew* is past tense for *know,* a word they had in the long -*o* sort. Remind them that when a syllable or a word that is one syllable ends with a long-vowel sound, it is called an *open syllable.* One way of labeling the open-syllable pattern is by labeling in a CV or CVV pattern, since *w* acts like a vowel.

Demonstrate

Demonstrate this sort as in the previous two sorts. There are three oddballs in this sort: *truth, do,* and *sew.* You will need to give your students a heads-up about the pronunciation of *sew.* Remind students that oddballs are usually words that have a spelling pattern associated with a different vowel sound than the one it actually has. After finding the oddballs in this sort, discuss their spelling pattern in terms of the vowel sound normally associated with that pattern, and then clarify the vowel sound they actually have.

CVC	CVV-ew	CVV-ue	
thumb	**new***	**due***	truth
plump	grew	flue	do
brush	chew	blue	sew
stuck	few	glue	
junk	flew	true	
trunk	knew*	clue	
	stew		
	blew*		
	dew*		

*homophones

Have your students **sort, check, reflect,** and **extend** this sort by completing the recommended standard weekly routines for sorts 19–24: Repeated Word Sorts, Writing Sorts, Speed Sorts, Word Hunts, and Blind or No-Peeking Sorts. You might dictate the sentence: *I knew he did not have a clue about the homework that was due in a few hours.*

More Difficult Words: (13) *crumb, tusk, husk, slump, snuff, shrewd, strewn, whew, screw, brew, hue, cruel, fuel.*

SORT 22   SHORT -*I* AND LONG -*I* (CVCe, VCC-*IGH*, AND OPEN SYLLABLE -*Y*)

This sort contains 23 words and four headers. Begin as usual by reading and discussing the meaning of the words, especially the homophones *write* and *right.* Next, display the short -*i* and long -*i* symbols with the pattern labels to head each of the four columns. Review the CVC pattern associated with the short -*i* sound and the CVCe pattern for the long -*i* sound. (If necessary, revisit sort 8.) Tell your students they will learn two new patterns for the long -*i* sound in this sort. Discuss how the *gh* of the *igh* pattern is silent but the *gh* signals that the *i* sound is long. Explain that we can label the *igh* pattern VCC, since the vowel *i* is followed by two consonants: the *g* and the *h*. Remind students that the open-syllable pattern in words like *why, cry,* and *sky* can be labeled CV, since the *y* acts as a vowel in these long -*i* words.

Demonstrate

Demonstrate the sort as in previous sorts. You might review the *qu* in the words *quick, quit,* and *quite.* As you sort, the word *since* may come up for discussion because it has a silent *e* at the end but does not have a long -*i* sound.

CVC	CVCe	VCC-*igh*	CV-y	
quick	**write***	**might**	**why**	since
quit	twice	high	cry	
	quite	night	sky	
	rise	bright	fly	
	white	fight	try	
		flight	shy	
		sight		
		sigh		
		right*		

* homophones

Have your students **sort, check, reflect,** and **extend** this sort by completing the recommended standard weekly routines for sorts 19–24. You might dictate the sentence: *Last night I had quite a fright!*

More Difficult Words: (15) *filth, risk, swift, twist, crime, prime, chime, lime, spice, lice, mite, fright, slight, thigh, sly.*

SORT 23   SHORT -*I* AND LONG -*I* (VCC) WITH SHORT -*O* AND LONG -*O* (VCC)

This sort contains 23 words and four headers and focuses on two additional VCC patterns for both the long -*i* and long -*o* sounds. These are contrasted with similar short-vowel patterns for both vowels. Because of the overlap in patterns, this can be a difficult sort. The oddball *lost* has a spelling pattern associated with both short and long -*o* words—as in *cost* versus *most*. *Lost* could be placed with short -*o* CVCC words or deemed an *oddball*. Since the patterns do overlap in this sort, it is best to sort first by sound, and then sort by patterns within each sound category.

CVCC	VCC	CVCC	VCC
film	**wild**	**loss**	**told**
fist	find	fond	most
	child	pond	cold
	kind	lost	both
	mind		roll
	blind		scold
	mild		gold
			post
			ghost
			fold

Have your students **sort, check, reflect,** and **extend** this sort by completing the recommended standard weekly routines for sorts 19–24.

More Difficult Words: (15) *mint, hint, sift, tilt, hind, wind, jolt, colt, bold, host, mold, volt, bolt, comb, cost.*

SORT 24   REVIEW OF LONG-VOWEL PATTERNS

This sort reviews the four long-vowel patterns that apply to all five long-vowel sounds for *a, e, i, o,* and *u.* The headers represent the patterns to be reviewed: VCC, CVVC, CVCe, and open-syllable patterns. There are 23 new words following these four familiar long-vowel patterns. Introduce the sort in a manner similar to sort 18.

CVCC	CVVC	CVCe	Open
sold	bleed	wave	glow
hold	steep	tone	crew
grind	sneak	slide	dry
bind	school	scene	crow
light	jail		drew
	soak		way
	pool		
	feast		

Review all the less common long-vowel patterns using words from sorts 19, 20, 21, 22, and 23.

SPELL CHECK 3
ASSESSMENT FOR LESS COMMON LONG-VOWEL PATTERNS

This assessment is administered as a writing sort. All of the words assessed have been presented previously in sorts 19–24. Photocopy page 58 for all students you wish to participate in the Spell Check. Say each word clearly, then ask your students to write it on lines provided under the correct pattern header. If you plan to grade this assessment, give one point for the proper placement of the word if it is written into the right category, and another point for the correct spelling of the word. These are the 20 words assessed:

1. gold	2. fruit	3. try
4. kind	5. pool	6. stay
7. child	8. chain	9. grow
10. light	11. sweet	12. few
13. rule	14. float	15. true
16. blame	17. spoon	18. drive
19. those	20. clue	

ă CVC	ā CVCe	āi CVVC
āy CVV	**lay**	**trade**
Spain	**glass**	stay
raise	grain	brave
play	clay	stand
slave	nail	tray
stray	gray	gain
taste	aid	hay
shape	past	pray

ŏ CVC	ō CVCe	ōa CVVC
ōw CVV	**froze**	**coal**
show	**stock**	slow
globe	coach	blow
grow	lose	Rome
roast	flow	throw
row	long	close
oat	mow	know
wrote	roam	loaf

SORT 21 *Short -u and Long -u (Open Syllable ew and ue)*

ŭ CVC	ēw CVV	ūe CVV
thumb	**new**	**due**
grew	truth	flue
plump	chew	do
blue	brush	glue
few	junk	true
stuck	flew	stew
knew	clue	blew
dew	trunk	sew

SORT 22 **Short -*i* and Long -*i* (CVCe, VCC-*igh*, and CV-Open Syllable-y)**

ĭ CVC	ī CVCe	īgh VCC
y = ī CV	**might**	**quick**
why	**write**	high
night	twice	quite
cry	bright	sky
quit	fight	fly
flight	sight	rise
try	since	white
sigh	shy	right

ĭ CVCC	ī VCC	ŏ CVCC
ō VCC	**wild**	**told**
film	**loss**	child
fond	lost	both
kind	roll	fist
cold	scold	gold
most	find	pond
post	fold	mild
blind	ghost	mind

CVCC	CVVC	CVCe
CV & CVV Open syllable	sold	bleed
wave	glow	hold
steep	tone	crew
grind	sneak	slide
dry	crow	bind
school	jail	soak
scene	drew	light
pool	way	feast

1. **CVCC**

_____

_____

_____

_____

_____

2. **CVCe**

_____

_____

_____

_____

_____

3. **CVVC**

_____

_____

_____

_____

4. **CV or CVV Open Syllable**

_____

_____

_____

_____

SORTS 25–30

R-Influenced Vowel Patterns

NOTES FOR THE TEACHER

Sorts 25–30 present the spelling patterns for *r*-influenced (or *r*-controlled) vowels for *a*, *e*, *i*, *o*, and *u*. Unfortunately, many students are stymied by *r*-influenced vowels and end up spelling simple words like *skirt*, SKURT; or even *girl* as GRIL. Fortunately, most *r*-influenced spelling patterns follow the same long-vowel patterns already studied, so this sequence of sorts will capitalize on this happy state of affairs by comparing and contrasting the short- and long-vowel patterns for the *r*-influenced words. There are many homophones among the *r*-influenced words and you will find that the use of meaning will help focus your students' attention on the vowel patterns that distinguish them. *Stair* and *stare*, *fair* and *fare*, *pair* and *pare* are all distinguishable by the long-vowel patterns learned in the earlier sorts in this supplement. Meaning will help straighten out even the most difficult of the *r*-influenced words—the "schwa plus *r*." The *schwa* is a vowel in an unstressed syllable such as the /uh/ sound in the first syllable of *about*, or a vowel in a single-syllable word that has been robbed of its own identity by the stronger sounds that surround it. Such is the case with words like *fir* and *fur*, *per* and *purr*. In all of these little words, the *r* robs the vowel of its own identity, making it impossible to tell what vowel is in the middle by the use of sound alone.

Sorts 25–30 are designed for middle-to-late within word pattern stage spellers. Most of the words in these sorts are on a third- to fourth-grade level. You might use the Spell Check on page 72 as a pretest to see which of your students are in need of these sorts. Students who spell most of the words on the Spell Check correctly may benefit from the study of some of the more difficult features introduced in sorts 31–49.

Each of these six sorts contains from 21 to 27 words plus column headers. Key words have been bolded and these should be placed at the top of each column. As always, key words are the most frequently occurring words of that particular spelling pattern. Oddballs are often words whose patterns violate the dominant pattern-to-sound correspondence. For example, the word *heard* is an oddball because it does not contain the long -*e* sound of other *ear* words like *hear* or *clear*. Many oddballs are homophones—they have a different pattern because they have a different meaning.

We recommend that you demonstrate the categorization of *r*-influenced spelling by first sorting by sound, and then sorting by patterns within each category of sound. While teacher-directed sorts are described here you may also choose to do open sorts as a first step. Remove the headers before giving students a copy of the words and ask them to discover categories on their own before sorting as a group.

Enlarge the sorts before duplicating for students. When possible, share books that contain a number of words with the targeted spelling feature. For example, *Wagon Wheels* (by Barbara Brennen) contains *r*-influenced words like *dirt, burn, third,* and *corn*. The *Story of Ferdinand* (by Munro Leaf) contains *cork* and *snort*.

STANDARD WEEKLY ROUTINES FOR USE WITH SORTS 25–30

1. **Repeated Work with Word Sorts:** Students sort their *r*-influenced word cards independently and with partners several times across the week. Students sort first by sound, and then by pattern within each category of sound.

2. **Writing Sorts and Word Study Notebooks:** Students record their word sorts by writing them into columns in their notebooks under the same key word that headed the columns of their word sort. Students write their reflections about what they learned about the spelling of these words after they have recorded their sort. See the homework form in the Appendix if you wish to assign additional sorts and writing sorts for homework.

3. **Write and Draw:** Since so many *r*-influenced patterns are homophones, this is an ideal time to reintroduce the idea of illustrating the meaning of these homophones with carefully done drawings and thoughtful sentences. Ask your students to pick five words from their weekly sort and draw a picture that will make their meaning clear. You will need to lay down some guidelines regarding the size and expectations for detail in these drawings. Also, you will need to model how to turn simple sentences into more elaborate ones. For example, use an overhead to show students how they can turn a simple sentence like, *I saw a hare* into a more elaborate version such as, *I saw a brown hare hopping through the forest* by asking questions like *What kind of hare?* or *Where did you see it?* Homophone illustrations and meaningful sentences can be collected to form a class homophone dictionary as described and illustrated in *WTW*.

4. **Speed Sorts:** Repeated word sorts can be timed using a stopwatch. Students try to sort faster and faster to try to beat their own time without sacrificing accuracy. Speed sorts help students become automatic in recognizing spelling patterns, and this translates into faster, more accurate word recognition.

5. **Word Hunts:** Students hunt through previously read material for additional exemplars of a pattern being studied.

6. **Dictated Sentences:** Compose a sentence containing some of the words in each lesson and have students write it to your dictation. Give them feedback about their spelling and mechanics.

7. **Blind or No-Peeking Sorts:** Blind or no-peeking sorts require students to think about words by sound and by pattern and to use the headers as models for analogy. See previous sorts for a description of this activity.

8. **Games and Other Activities:** Create games and activities such as those in Chapter 6 of *WTW* or download them ready made from the *WTW* CD-ROM. The game Treasure from the *WTW* CD-ROM is one we highly recommend for extended practice with *r*-influenced vowel patterns.

9. **Assessment:** An assessment of *r*-influenced homophones may be found on page 72. Note that this assessment requires students to recognize the spelling pattern associated with a particular *meaning*.

SORT 25   *AR, ARE, AIR*
Demonstrate

There are 23 words in this *r*-influenced sort. Read and discuss the words before sorting, paying particular attention to the homophones (see asterisked words below). When you discuss these words again after the sorting, you and your students will probably conclude that all of these words are influenced by the sound of the /r/ but that they still work the same way as most short- and long-vowel patterns do.

First, sort the words into two columns by *sound:* short -*r* words that sound like /ar/ in the middle, and long -*r* words that sound like the word *air* in the middle. All of the words will fit into one of these two categories. Next, discuss the spelling patterns of most of the short -*r* words. All but one are spelled with *ar* in the middle, just as it sounds. The exception, *heart*, could be considered an oddball since it sounds like a short -*r* word but is not spelled with *ar*. Tell students that there is a homophone partner for the word *heart* spelled with an *ar*—*hart*—an old-fashioned word for a male deer. The word *heart* has a different spelling pattern since the *ar* was already taken. If you like, add the word *hart* to the short -*r* group by using the blank template in the back of the book.

Next, discuss the spelling patterns of the long-*r* group. Many patterns should be familiar to students, particularly the *are* and *air* patterns. Display the *are* and *air* pattern headers and sort the long -*r* group by these patterns. The ones that do not fit may be considered oddballs. Ask if they notice any recurring spelling pattern among the oddballs. *Bear, wear,* and *pear* are all spelled with an *ear* pattern but have a long -*a*, not a long -*e*, sound. The pattern in the word *where* is unique but necessary since *ware* and *wear* are already taken. Sort 25 should look something like this:

ar	*are*	*air*	*oddball*
part	**care**	**hair***	pear*
start	pare*	fair*	wear*
harm	stare*	pair*	bear*
sharp	square*	chair	where*
dark	bare*	stair	heart*
shark	fare*		
	hare		

* homophones

Sort, Check, Reflect, and Extend

Have your students sort their own word cards, check their sorts by reading down each column to check for consistency in sound and pattern, then record their sort in their word study notebooks declaring what they have learned in a written reflection. **Extend** this sort with Write and Draw activities and other standard weekly routines. Do not forget about the game Treasure from the *WTW* CD-ROM.

More Difficult Words: (15) *hart, harp, barb, scar, lark, arch, glare, ware, flare, rare, snare, spare, blare, flair, lair.*

SORT 26   *ER, EAR, EER*

This sort contains 23 *r*-influenced *e* words. Introduce the sort in a manner similar to sort 25. The oddballs *earth, heard,* and *learn* all contain the *ear* pattern but do not have the long -*e* sound associated with that pattern in words like *ear* or *hear.* Be sure to discuss the meaning of the word *heard* as distinct from its homophone partner *herd,* and point out the *hear* inside of *heard* as a spelling-meaning connection. You might discuss the change in verb tense between *hear* and *heard* and use them both in meaningful sentences.

er	*ear*	*eer*	*oddball*
her	**ear**	**deer***	earth
perch	fear	steer	heard*
herd*	spear	cheer	learn
fern	clear	peer	
germ	rear		
clerk	dear*		
term	year		
	near		
	beard		

* homophones

NOTE: *The words* nerve, serve, *or* terse *may be encountered in a word hunt and may be placed in the oddball category. The final* e *in these words merits some discussion so as to be distinguished from the silent* -e *of the CVCe long-vowel pattern. This feature is taught directly in sort 40.*

More Difficult Words: (10) *herb, perk, stern, jerk, sear, queer, sneer, leer, yearn, swear.*

SORT 27   *IR, IRE, IER*

There are 24 words and three headers in this *r*-influenced *i* sort. Introduce the sort in a manner similar to the previous two sorts. The meaning and spelling of the oddball *fur* should be discussed and contrasted with its homophone partner *fir.* You may prefer to categorize the words *drier, pliers, flier,* and *crier* as oddballs, too, as these words are derived from another form of the word. These *ier* words should be discussed in terms of the meaning of their base forms and the spelling changes that occur when changing the verb (*dry, fly, ply, cry*) to a noun (*drier, pliers, flier, crier*). Be sure to use these words in meaningful sentences. Most students will be unfamiliar with the meaning of the verb *ply* and may not know what *pliers* are, so you might want to bring in your toolbox! The word *higher* is not included in this but may come up as a homophone partner to *hire.* The words *whirl, twirl,* and *swirl* are very difficult words because of the presence of the /w/ sound at the beginning and because of the *l* in addition to the *r* at the end. Also, these words all have similar meanings that will require discussion and maybe even physical demonstration. Happy twirling!

ir	*ire*	*ier*	
bird	**fire**	**drier**	fur*
first	wire	pliers	
dirt	tire	flier	
third	hire*	crier	
girl			
birth			
shirt			
fir*			
whirl			
swirl			
thirst			
chirp			
skirt			
stir			
twirl			

*homophone

NOTE: *It is impossible to hear the short -i sound apart from the /r/ sound in the ir words because the sound of /r/ includes the vowel. Because r-blends like the* fr, gr, *or* br *in easy words like* frog, grab, *and* brick *are very common, some students may persist spelling* first *as FRIST,* girl *as GRIL,* bird *as BRID. If this problem persists, you might extend this sort by comparing common r-blends to these short -r words (*grip *versus* girl; drip *versus* dirt, *etc.). See Chapter 6 in* WTW *for details.*

More Difficult Words: (10) *firm, sir, whirr, sire, spire, mire, higher, liar, friar, frier.*

Sort, Check, Reflect, and Extend

Have your students sort their own word cards and check their sorts by reading down each column to check for consistency in sound and pattern. Have them record their sort in their word study notebooks and declare what they have learned in a written reflection. **Extend** this sort with Write and Draw activities and other standard weekly routines. Additional *r*-influenced sorts may be found in the Appendix of *WTW*.

SORT 28   OR, ORE, OAR

R-influenced *o* words do not have the short and long distinction in sound that the *r*-influenced patterns for *a, e,* and *i* do. The vowel sound is pronounced /or/ whether the word is long or short. The vowel sounds in *fork, store,* and *roar* are all the same. *R*-influenced *o* words have the further distinction of having a *schwa plus r* sound that occurs in words that start with *w*—words like *word, work,* or *worm.* In *w* plus *or* words the vowel sound is robbed of its identity because of the stronger sounds of the *w* and *r* on either side. Introduce this sort by the patterns *or, ore, oar,* and *w + or.* Be sure to discuss how the sound of *or* changes after *w.* The oddballs in this sort also have the /or/ sound but have different patterns—as in *four, floor,* and *poor.* There are also six homophones in this sort, but only one homophone in the pair is included. In each case, the homophone partner is a more difficult word. The partners are included in the list of More Difficult Words below.

or	*ore*	*oar*	*w + or*	
form	**shore**	**board***	**word**	four*
fork	store	roar	work	floor
horn	more	oar*	world	poor*
north	tore	soar*	worm	
corn	wore			
storm	horse*			
*homophones				

More Difficult Words: (18) *chord, ford, fort, pork, sworn, for, scorn, sore, swore, forge, gorge, ore, coarse, bored, worse, pour, fourth, court.*

SORT 29   UR, URE, UR-E

There are only 21 words in this *r*-influenced *u* sort because it is more difficult than the previous four sorts in this series. The words themselves are harder so you must be careful to bring them to life through enriched discussion and by providing robust examples. Many students may not have heard of the words *lure, churn,* or *surf.* In addition, there is considerable variation in the pronunciation of some of the *ure* words like *pure* and *cure.* Some may pronounce these words as two syllables as in *pee-your* for *pure.* You may find some students placing *pure* and *cure* in the oddball column while others may put them with the other *ure* words like *sure* and *lure.* Either way is fine. You will need to discuss the final *e* in the words *curve, nurse, purse,* and *curse* and distinguish the *ur-e* pattern from the CVCe long-vowel pattern. You could keep these words in their own *ur-e* category because of their unique spelling pattern, or you could put them with the *ur* group since they share the same *schwa-plus-r* sound in the middle. To work out these issues, we recommend introducing this sort in a two-column **sound sort** first.

Demonstrate the **sound sort,** which may look like this:

turn	*sure*
burn	lure
hurt	pure
curl	cure
church	
hurl	
burst	
churn	
surf*	
purr*	
curb	
turkey	
purple	
curve	
nurse	
purse	
curse	

*homophones

Follow this with a **pattern sort** which will look like this:

ur	*ure*	*ur-e*	*oddball*
turn	**sure**	**curve**	
burn	lure	nurse	
hurt	pure	purse	
curl	cure	curse	
church			
hurl			
burst			
churn			
surf*			
purr*			
curb			
turkey			
purple			

*homophones

More Difficult Words: (5) *blurt, lurch, spurt, burr, purge.*

SORT 30   REVIEW OF *AR*, *SCHWA-PLUS-R*, AND *OR*

The sounds and patterns of the previous five sorts are reviewed in this sound sort that presents 24 words in three categories. The words *serve* and *nerve* may be categorized as oddballs due to their final *e,* or they may be grouped with the *schwa-plus-r* words that have the same sound. All but one of the words are new words that follow the same sound and patterns presented in sorts 25–29. The word *horse* is repeated to complete the homophone pair *hoarse* and *horse.* The homophones *boar* and *bore* will require discussion. Display the headers *ar*, *schwa + r*, and *or*, then introduce the sound sort in a manner similar to sort 28.

ar	*Schwa + r*	*or*	
jar	earn	torn	serve
hard	search	snort	nerve
yard	pearl	hoarse*	
march	worth	horse*	
	worst	core	
	spur	chore	
	sir	boar*	
	lurk	bore*	
		score	
		snore	

*homophones

More Difficult Words: (4) *war, warn, warp, ward.*

SPELL CHECK 4
ASSESSMENT FOR *R*-INFLUENCED VOWELS

This assessment is presented in a word recognition format and checks for the recognition of the correct spelling pattern of 20 *r*-influenced words. The Spell Check assesses the short and long *r*-influenced vowel sounds as well as the *schwa-plus-r* sound. Six homophones are included to assess student knowledge of the spelling patterns that differentiate their word meanings. All of the words assessed have been studied before in sorts 25–30. Photocopy page 72 for all students you wish to participate in the Spell Check. Name each picture, then read the sentence that goes with each picture (see below). You may need the sentences to be sure students know which meaning the pictures are targeting, especially for the homophones. Tell your students to circle the word under each picture that matches the meaning of the sentence and that contains the correct spelling pattern.

1. **Bird.** A **bird** is a warm-blooded, egg-laying, feathered vertebrate with wings. **Bird.**
2. **Thorn.** A **thorn** is a sharp, spiny point that sticks out of a plant stem and can prick your finger. **Thorn.**
3. **Shirt.** A **shirt** is a piece of clothing for the upper part of the body typically having a collar, sleeves, and a front opening. **Shirt.**
4. **Jar.** A **jar** is a glass or ceramic container with a wide mouth, usually without handles; is cylinder-shaped, and used to store things like honey. **Jar.**
5. **Tire.** A **tire** is a covering for a wheel, usually made out of rubber. **Tire.**
6. **Fire.** They learned how to start a **fire** by rubbing two sticks together. **Fire.**
7. **Heart.** Most valentines are in the shape of a **heart. Heart.**
8. **Deer.** A male **deer** grows antlers and is sometimes called a buck. **Deer.**
9. **Horn.** A **horn** is a musical instrument such as a trumpet. **Horn.**
10. **Worm.** **Worms** are invertebrate animals that often have no arms or legs. **Worms.**
11. **Four.** The number **four** comes after the number three. **Four.**
12. **Chair.** A **chair** is a piece of furniture that makes it possible for people to sit. **Chair.**
13. **First. First** corresponds in order to the number 1. **First.**
14. **Yarn. Yarn** is a long strand of twisted thread made of a fiber such as wool, and is used in weaving or knitting. **Yarn.**
15. **Pliers. Pliers** are a type of tool used for holding, bending, or cutting. **Pliers.**
16. **Pear.** A **pear** is a type of fruit that is eaten like an apple. **Pear.**
17. **Corn. Corn** is a type of grain or cereal plant that bears seeds or kernels on large ears. **Corn.**
18. **Horse.** A **horse** is a large hoofed animal with a shorthaired coat, a long mane, and a long tail; and is used for riding and carrying heavy loads. **Horse.**
19. **Hare.** A **hare** looks like a rabbit with long ears, large hind feet, and legs that are made for jumping. **Hare.**
20. **Fork.** A **fork** is a three- or four-pronged utensil used for serving or eating food. **Fork.**

ar	***are***	***air***
oddball	**care**	**hair**
part	fair	start
harm	pare	chair
wear	sharp	pair
stare	where	dark
square	hare	pear
heart	shark	fare
bear	stair	bare

er	*ear*	*eer*
oddball	**her**	**deer**
ear	perch	fear
spear	steer	earth
herd	clear	rear
cheer	heard	peer
fern	dear	year
near	learn	germ
clerk	beard	term

SORT 27   *ir/ire/ier*

ir	*ire*	*ier*
bird	fire	drier
third	girl	birth
tire	flier	shirt
fir	whirl	hire
pliers	swirl	thirst
chirp	crier	skirt
stir	twirl	wire
dirt	fur	first

Words Their Way: Word Sorts for Within Word Pattern Spellers © 2004 by Prentice-Hall, Inc.

68

SORT 28   *or/ore/oar*

or	*ore*	*oar*
w + or	**form**	**shore**
board	**word**	four
horn	store	roar
work	north	more
soar	world	floor
corn	fork	wore
worm	poor	storm
horse	tore	oar

ur	*ure*	*ur–e*
oddball	**turn**	**sure**
curve	pure	burn
hurt	curl	church
lure	nurse	cure
purse	hurl	burst
churn	curse	surf
purr	curb	
turkey	purple	

ar	*ər*	*or*
jar	earn	torn
search	snort	hoarse
hard	pearl	horse
worth	core	serve
worst	chore	boar
nerve	bore	yard
spur	score	lurk
march	snore	sir

1. burd berd bird	2. thorne thorn thourn
3. shirt shert shurt	4. jar jare jaw
5. tier tire tyre	6. fier flyer fire
7. hart heart hairt	8. deer dear dere
9. horn horne hoarn	10. warm worm wurm
11. fore four for	12. chair chayre chare
13. ferst first furst	14. yawn yaun yarn
15. plyers plires pliers	16. pare pair pear
17. coarn corn corne	18. hoarse house horse
19. hair haer hare	20. fourk furk fork

Words Their Way: Word Sorts for Within Word Pattern Spellers © 2004 by Prentice-Hall, Inc.

SORTS 31–35

Diphthongs and Other Ambiguous Vowel Sounds

NOTES FOR THE TEACHER

Sorts 31–35 deal with the spellings of a variety of other vowel sounds that are not influenced by *r* and are neither long nor short. These other vowel sounds usually involve two vowels (like the double *o* in *book* or the *au* in *cause*) or a vowel and a second letter that has some vowel-like qualities. The /l/ and /w/ sounds are examples of consonants that influence the sound of the vowel in an ambiguous way that is difficult to describe (*salt, crowd*). Often the influence of the second letter creates a *glide,* where the vowel sound slithers from one sound to another, as in the word *boy,* where the vowel starts out like the vowel sound in *door* but slides into a long *-e* sound at the very end (*bo-ee*). These glides, or diphthongs, can be tricky.

The study of diphthongs and other ambiguous vowels is appropriate for students in the late within word pattern stage who have already mastered most of the common and less common short- and long-vowel patterns as well as the *r*-influenced patterns presented in the previous sorts. Diphthongs and other ambiguous vowels are usually the last vowel patterns to be learned in the within word pattern stage. We place them here, after the *r*-influenced vowels, so that all of the vowel patterns are learned in a planned sequence. However, they could just as easily be studied after the complex consonants presented in the next set of sorts.

In *WTW* we recommend highlighting a new spelling feature by comparing it to what students already know—in this case, long- and short-vowel patterns. This approach may be accomplished here by combining sort 31 with sort 20 and conducting a three-column *sound sort:* short *-o* sounds, long *-o* sounds, and other *-o* sounds that are neither long nor short—in this case, the diphthong /oyee/. A pattern sort for the other category would follow this initial sound sort. For expediency, however, sort 31 immediately presents the two most common spellings for the diphthong /oyee/ (*oi* and *oy*) in a pattern sort.

The remaining sorts in this sequence alternate between *pattern sorts* for diphthongs (gliding vowel sounds) and *sound sorts* for the other ambiguous vowel sounds. Sort 32, for example, uses a sound sort to focus students' attention on the difference between the long *-u* sound in words like *boot* and *noon* and the other back vowel sound in words like *book* or *crook*—all spelled with the same double *-o* pattern. Sort 33 uses a pattern sort to highlight the two most common spellings of the /aw/ sound: *aw* and *au*. Sort 34 returns to a sound sort to compare and contrast the broad *-a* sound in words like *wash* and *watch* with the /all/ sound in words like *walk* and *bald*. Sort 35 presents a pattern sort that features the two most common spelling patterns for the /ow/ sound: *ow* and *ou*.

We recommend recycling sorts 31–35 to review all of these close back vowel sounds before the Spell Check 5—an assessment of 24 diphthongs and other ambiguous vowels studied in sorts 31–35. The review can be a giant pattern sort or a two-step sort that sorts first by sound and then by pattern within categories of sound.

Diphthongs and other ambiguous vowels are not as common as short and long or *r*-influenced vowel patterns, so there are words in each sort that may be unfamiliar to students. This is alright as long as students can read the words and are familiar with the majority of them. Homophones as well as words whose meanings are probably not known are asterisked. These word meanings must be introduced, discussed, and used in meaningful contexts throughout the week.

Use the Spell Check 5 on page 85 as a pretest to make sure your students need and can do these sorts. Students who spell all of the words on the Spell Check correctly may benefit from the study of the more difficult features introduced later in this supplement. Students who are obviously frustrated in attempting the spelling of the words in the Spell Check should start with easier sorts. Use the spelling assessments in Chapter 2 of *WTW* to pinpoint different starting points for different students.

Each of the sorts in this series contains approximately 25 words plus two column headers. Key words have been bolded and these should be placed at the top of each column. As always, key words are the most frequently occurring words of that particular spelling pattern. Oddballs are either high-frequency words whose patterns violate the dominant pattern-to-sound correspondence (e.g., *laugh*) or are words that have an unusual pattern for that particular sound. Some of these patterns form a consistent category of their own. For example, the high-frequency words *should, would,* and *could* have an unusual spelling pattern for that particular sound, but these three words form a small but consistent pattern-to-sound category by themselves.

If possible, share books and poems that contain some words with the same targeted spelling features. For example, the traditional song *I Wish I Was a Mole in the Ground* (Tashjian, 1941) has many diphthong sounds for *ou* and *ow,* and such books as *Minnie and Moo Go to the Moon* (by Denys Cazet) and *Midnight on the Moon* (by Mary Pope Osborn) contain many examples of *ou, ow,* and *oi.*

STANDARD WEEKLY ROUTINES FOR USE WITH SORTS 31–35

1. **Repeated Work with Word Sorts:** Students sort their own word cards several times independently and with partners after the sort has been introduced as described in each lesson below. Additional practice doing word sorts can occur through homework. See the homework form in the Appendix.
2. **Writing Sorts and Word Study Notebooks:** Students record their word sorts by writing them into columns in their notebooks under the same key words that headed the word sorts. You might ask students to choose 5 to 10 words to use in thoughtful sentences and coach them through the elaboration process described in Write and Draw on page 60. Do not allow students to use more than two spelling words per sentence, however, or you are likely to get nonsense.
3. **Word-O:** Ask students to conduct a word operation on three to four words as described on page 30. Add, subtract, or substitute consonants to make a new word. Start with the word *foil,* for example, and subtract the *f* to get *oil.* Add a *b* to *oil* to get *boil.* Add an *r* to get *broil.* Have students record their word operations in their word study notebooks by writing the new word to the right of the original word. Tell them to underline the letters that were changed in their operation.
4. **Speed Sorts:** Have students time themselves with a stopwatch as they sort their words into categories. After obtaining a baseline speed, they repeat the sort several times and try to beat their own time. Repeated, timed speed sorts help students internalize spelling patterns and develop automatic word recognition.

5. **Word Hunts:** Word hunts help students see the connection between reading and spelling. Have students search through books they have already read to find additional exemplars of diphthongs and other ambiguous vowel patterns. Have students record the words they find in the proper column in their word study notebook and share them with the group when they meet.

6. **Dictated Sentences:** Prepare a sentence that contains several of your word study words and have students write it to your dictation. Discuss spelling and mechanics.

7. **Blind or No-Peeking Sorts:** Blind or no-peeking sorts and no-peeking writing sorts require students to think about words by sound and by pattern and to use the headers as models for analogy. Blind or no-peeking sorts are a great way to practice for spelling tests.

8. **Games and Other Activities:** Additional sorts for diphthongs and other vowel digraphs may be found in the Appendix of *WTW* on pages 378 and 390. See the activities section at the end of Chapter 6 for games and other extensions.

9. **Assessment:** To assess students' weekly mastery, ask them to spell the words and categorize them by sound and by pattern. An assessment of the diphthongs and other ambiguous vowels presented in sorts 31–35 may be found on page 85: *Spell Check 5 Diphthongs and Other Ambiguous Vowels.*

SORT 31   *OI, OY*

This is a pattern sort for the diphthong /oyee/. Before demonstrating the sort, be sure to read and discuss the meanings of the asterisked words. If you feel there are too many unfamiliar words, eliminate some. Boldface words are the most frequently occurring words in that pattern and could be used as key words to head the column. The words *noise, choice,* and *voice* could be sorted with the *oi* words, or placed as oddballs because of their final *-e.* Remind your students that the final *-e* in these words signals the pronunciation of the last consonant sound. For example, the final *-e* in *noise* tells us that the final /s/ is pronounced more like a /z/. Similarly, the final *-e* in *choice* and *voice* signals that the final /c/ is pronounced like an /s/ rather than the hard sound of *c*. The words *enjoy* and *decoy* are two-syllable words and students may need help in eyeballing the *oy* pattern in the accented syllable.

   Demonstrate, sort, check, reflect, and then **extend** as usual by following the standard weekly routines previously described. As you and your students reflect on this sort, help them form generalizations by asking which spelling pattern is used when the /oyee/ sound is at the very end of a word. Which spelling pattern is used when the /oyee/ sound is in the middle of a word?

oi	*oy*	
point	**boy**	noise
join	soy	choice
soil	joy	voice
spoil	coy*	
coil	toy	
foil*	ploy*	
moist	decoy*	
joint	enjoy	
boil		
coin		
broil		
toil*		
oil		
hoist*		

*difficult words that require discussion

SORT 32   *OO, OO*

This is a sound sort that compares the long *-u* sound in words like *soon* and *root* to another back vowel sound in words like *good* and *foot*. All of them are spelled with a double *-o*. The words *could*, *would*, and *should* are oddballs because they have the same vowel sound as the words *stood* and *good*, but are spelled differently. Conveniently, *would* and *wood* are homophones so you can discuss the necessity for having different spelling patterns to reflect their different meanings. The word *root* is also a homophone, though its partner, *route*, is not included in this sort. Feel free to add it by using the blank template in the back of this book. It will be interesting to see where your students would put it. Boldface words are the most frequently occurring words in that pattern and could be used as key words to head the columns.

Demonstrate, sort, check, reflect, and then extend this word sort by following the standard weekly routines previously described.

oo = ū	*ŏo*	
soon	**good**	*oddball*
cool	brook	could
fool	crook	would*
noon	wood*	should
groom	hood	
root*	stood	
tool	hook	
troop	foot	
hoop	wool	
stool	soot	
proof		
roost		

*homophone

More Difficult Words: (10) *coop, brood, spool, doom, gloom, spook, zoom, loot, rook, nook.*

SORT 33   *AW, AU*

This is a pattern sort for the /aw/ sound of *aw* and *au*. Before demonstrating the sort, be sure to read and discuss the meanings of the words, especially the asterisked ones. For *vault*, you might refer to Gringots (the bank) in *Harry Potter*. Boldface words are the most frequently occurring words in that pattern and could be used as key words. The word *laugh* is an oddball because it has the *au* pattern characteristic of the /aw/ sound, but it has a short *-a* sound instead.

If you decide that this two-pattern sort is too easy for your students, consider bringing in the *ou* words from the next sort to increase the number of pattern contrasts (*bought, thought, brought,* and so on).

Demonstrate, sort, check, reflect, and then extend as usual by following the standard weekly routines previously described. As you and your students reflect on this sort, help them form generalizations by asking if there is a spelling pattern that is used more often when the /aw/ sound is at the very end of a word. Is there a spelling pattern that is never used when the /aw/ sound is at the end of a word? Are there any other recurring letter patterns within each category worth noting? Which pattern has more *en*s or *el*s at the very end of words?

aw	au	oddball
saw	**caught**	laugh
paw	cause	
straw	fault	
lawn	pause	
claw	sauce	
draw	taught	
yawn	haul	
hawk	launch	
crawl	vault*	
dawn	haunt	
shawl*		
drawn		
raw		
law		
*difficult		

More Difficult Words: (7) *bawl, fawn, sprawl, thaw, flaw, maul, haunch.*

SORT 34   *WA, AL, OU*

This sound sort contrasts the broad -*a* in words like *wash* and *watch,* the /all/ sound in words like *small* and *salt,* and another /aw/ sound in words like *bought* and *fought.* In some dialects, the words *bought* and *fought* are pronounced more like the /ô/ sound in *more* and *store.* Either way is fine. There is no one correct pronunciation and English speakers of all dialects must associate their own pronunciation with the same spelling patterns. Even if some students think that *bought, thought,* and *brought* have the same vowel sound as *salt* and *talk,* they can still sort by pattern. Watch out for the word *walk.* Students will want to put it with the *wa* words but it does not have the same broad -*a* sound as *watch.* Note that two two-syllable words are used—*almost* and *also,* but these are very high-frequency words that students at this level should definitely learn how to read and spell if they do not know already.

   Demonstrate, sort, check, reflect, and then **extend** as usual by following the standard weekly routines previously described. As you and your students reflect on this sort, help them form generalizations by asking what is the same about many of the words within a category in terms of their spelling patterns.

wa	al	ou
watch	**small**	**thought**
wash	almost	bought
wand	also	brought
wasp	walk	fought
swap	tall	ought
swat	salt	cough
	calm	
	talk	
	stalk	
	bald	
	chalk	
	stall	

More Difficult Words: (7) *water, psalm, palm, halt, sought, trough, though.*

SORT 35   *OU, OW*

This pattern sort contrasts the two major spelling patterns for the /ow/ sound in words like *sound* and *crowd: ou* and *ow.* These words should all be familiar to your students, but read and discuss them before demonstrating the sort anyway. Since the *ou* words in the previous sort (sort 34) were associated with the /aw/ sound, explicitly tell your students that the *ou* pattern in this sort represents the /ow/ sound this time. Oddballs include two words with *ou* patterns associated with yet another vowel sound (*tough, rough*), and one word with an *ow* pattern associated with the long -o sound. You might want to recycle your old long -o words with the *ow* pattern from sort 20 just to keep your students on their toes.

    Demonstrate, sort, check, reflect, and then **extend** as usual by following the standard weekly routines previously described. If your students go on word hunts in search of more words that contain *ou* and *ow* patterns for the /ow/ sound, they might find the words *house, mouse, ounce,* or *pounce.* These words can be added to the *ou* group since they do have the /ow/ sound spelled with the *ou* pattern. However, you may need to discuss the role of the final -e in those words, as you did for the words *choice* and *voice* back in sort 31. Your students may also find two other high-frequency exceptions—*though* and *through*—which can both be placed in the oddball column since neither of them have the /ow/ sound. Help your students make generalizations about these pattern-to-sound relationships by asking them to reflect on the preponderance of rhyming words in certain categories.

ou	*ow*	*oddball*
sound	**brown**	tough
cloud	clown	rough
found	growl	grown
ground	howl	
pound	owl	
shout	crown	
count	drown	
mouth	frown	
south	gown	
couch	plow	
scout	town	

    Collect more *ou* and *ow* words and then sort them by rhyming families: *found, sound, pound—out, shout, pout—ouch, couch, pouch—house, mouse, louse—town, clown, brown—owl, howl, growl—now, plow, cow,* and so on.

More Difficult Words: (10) *foul, drought, stout, doubt, fowl, prowl, scowl, brow, vow, touch.*

SPELL CHECK 5
ASSESSMENT FOR DIPHTHONGS AND OTHER AMBIGUOUS VOWELS

Before assessing your students' mastery of the spelling patterns associated with diphthongs and other ambiguous vowel sounds, give them a chance to review. Combine all of the word cards from sorts 31–35. Sort them by sound first, and then by pattern within categories of sound.

    This assessment is presented in a writing sort format and checks for correct spelling of 24 of the 125 words sorted in sorts 31–35. All of the words assessed have been studied before in these previous sorts. Photocopy and enlarge page 85 for all students you wish to participate in the Spell Check. Say each word clearly and ask your students to write the word in the box labeled with the correct vowel pattern. For example, if you call the word *calm*, students would write *calm* in the third box labeled with an *al* at the top, since the word *calm* is spelled with an *al* in the middle. If you are grading this Spell Check, consider giving one point for writing the word in the correct category and another point for the correct spelling of the entire word.

Call out the words in the following order and use each word in a sentence to make sure your students understand what word you are saying. Say each word once, use it in a sentence, then say it again:

1. crawl, 2. chalk, 3. growl, 4. joy, 5. spoil, 6. mouth, 7. caught, 8. point, 9. taught, 10. drawn, 11. couch, 12. stalk, 13. drown, 14. brought, 15. cloud, 16. gown, 17. yawn, 18. calm, 19. haul, 20. noise, 21. thought, 22. rough, 23. fault, 24. could

Allow time for students to reorganize their words if needed. The words *brought*, *thought*, *rough*, and *could* might also be squeezed into the *ou* box since this is a pattern-writing sort. Otherwise, the answer sheet will look like this:

1. **aw**	2. **au**	3. **al**	
crawl	caught	chalk	brought
drawn	taught	stalk	thought
yawn	haul	calm	rough
	fault		could

4. **ow**	5. **ou**	6. **oy**	7. **oi**
growl	mouth	joy	spoil
drown	couch		point
gown	cloud		noise

oi	*oy*	**boy**
point	join	soil
noise	soy	spoil
coy	coil	joy
foil	moist	joint
boil	toy	voice
coin	broil	ploy
toil	oil	hoist
enjoy	decoy	choice

SORT 32   Double o (Long -u and Schwa Sound)

OO = ū	ŏŏ	**soon**
good	cool	crook
fool	wood	could
noon	groom	hood
root	stood	tool
hook	troop	foot
hoop	should	brook
stool	proof	wool
would	soot	roost

aw	*au*	**saw**
caught	lawn	cause
paw	straw	fault
law	claw	sauce
taught	draw	laugh
haul	pause	yawn
haunt	hawk	crawl
dawn	launch	vault
shawl	drawn	raw

Words Their Way: Word Sorts for Within Word Pattern Spellers © 2004 by Prentice-Hall, Inc.

wa	*al*	*ou*
watch	**small**	**thought**
walk	salt	wash
tall	calm	bought
wand	talk	stalk
bald	wasp	fought
swap	chalk	stall
ought	swat	brought
cough	also	almost

ou	*ow*	**sound**
brown	cloud	clown
growl	found	howl
tough	ground	crown
owl	pound	shout
drown	rough	frown
gown	mouth	plow
south	grown	couch
scout	town	count

Spell Check 5 Sorts 31–35 Diphthongs and Other Ambiguous Vowels   Name _____

1. aw	2. au	3. al	

4. ow	5. ou	6. oy	7. oi

Words Their Way: Word Sorts for Within Word Pattern Spellers © 2004 by Prentice-Hall, Inc.

SORTS 36–42

Beginning and Ending Complex Consonants and Consonant Clusters

NOTES FOR THE TEACHER

Sorts 36–42 mark a shift in focus from vowel patterns to consonant patterns. Sorts 36–39 target complex consonants at the beginning of words while sorts 40–42 focus on complex consonants at the ends of words. Shifting focus from vowel patterns back to the beginning of words may cause some initial confusion, but with an increase in orthographic knowledge comes a corresponding increase in flexibility. Since your students have now internalized the vowel patterns studied in the previous sections of this supplement, they are probably reading more difficult text and encountering new features such as silent consonants at the beginning (*knife*, *wrong*, *gnat*) and strange-looking consonant clusters like *tch* and *dge* at the ends of words (*catch*, *lodge*). To lead your students to higher levels of word knowledge, these features are worth a few weeks of study.

The study of complex consonants begins with a look at silent consonants at the beginning of words like *knight*, *wreath*, and *gnat*. A few of these words may be more difficult than the third- to fourth-grade words previously sorted, so the importance of bringing the meanings of these words to life is paramount, especially for our English Language Learners (ELLs).

The study of silent consonants is followed by two sorts that revisit more advanced forms of consonant blends and consonant digraphs; specifically, triple *r*-blends like the *scr*, *str*, and *spr* (*screen*, *strong*, *spring*) and triple-letter consonant digraph-plus-*r*-blend combinations like *thr* and *shr* (*through*, *shred*). Since these triple *r*-blends and digraph-*r*-blend combinations involve that slippery *r* again, you might want to combine sorts 37 and 38 with some of the *r*-influenced words from sorts 25–30. The study of these triple *r*-blends and digraph-plus-*r*-blend combinations might be accomplished in one or two weeks depending on your students' previous experience and knowledge. See Chapter 6 in *WTW* for additional suggestions for pacing.

Although sort 39 (hard and soft *C* and *G*) still focuses on consonants at the beginning of words, hard and soft *C* and *G* are determined by the vowel that follows, so this sort segues nicely into the study of complex consonants at the end of words that are also determined by the vowel sound. Sort 40 shifts the focus to the ends of words and examines words ending in *ce* versus *se* as in *peace* versus *please*. Since this feature was encountered several times during the study of diphthongs and other ambiguous vowel sounds (e.g., *choice, noise*), you may wish to skip sort 40 altogether.

Sorts 41 and 42 deal with the complex consonants *tch* and *dge* at the end of words like *match* and *lodge*. This feature continues to bewilder students in the middle-to-late within word pattern stage who use but confuse *ch* and *tch*, *ge* and *dge*. They may spell *pitch*, PICH; or *lodge*, LOGE. Fortunately these consonant patterns are determined by vowel sounds, so students return to familiar word study routines in sorts 41 and 42 such as sorting words by vowel sounds.

This section is punctuated by the inclusion of three Spell Checks representing the three features examined in this planned sequence. You could also use these Spell Checks as a pretest to see if your students truly need each set of sorts. As always, we recommend that you assess all of your students with one of the *WTW* spelling inventories to make sure you are matching your word study instruction to student needs appropriately.

The study of complex consonants is appropriate for students in the middle-to-late within word pattern stage who have already mastered most of the common and less common short- and long-vowel patterns as well as the *r*-influenced patterns presented earlier in this supplement. We place them here, after the study of diphthongs and other ambiguous vowel sounds, so that vowel sounds are thoroughly understood before examining how they also affect consonants. However, complex consonants could just as easily be studied before the series on diphthongs and other ambiguous vowel sounds.

Each of the sorts in this series contains 23 or 24 words plus three or four column headers. Key words have been bolded and these should be placed at the top of each column. As always, key words are the most frequently occurring words of that particular spelling pattern. Oddballs are either homophones with a completely different pattern (*ring* versus *wring*) or provide a segue to the next feature to be studied. For example, the word *squirrel* is included as an oddball in the triple *r*-blend set for *scr, str,* and *spr* to bridge into the *squ* feature in the next sort. Some oddballs are high-frequency words that violate the dominant pattern-to-sound correspondence. If possible, share books, songs, or poems that use some words that contain the targeted spelling feature. *Stone Fox* (by John Reynolds Gardiner) uses many complex consonant blends like *strength, stronger,* and *straight*.

STANDARD WEEKLY ROUTINES FOR USE WITH SORTS 36–42

1. **Repeated Work with Word Sorts:** Students should sort their own word cards several times independently and with partners after the sort has been introduced as described in each lesson below. Words can be stored in an envelope or baggie.

2. **Writing Sorts and Word Study Notebooks:** Students should record their word sorts by writing them into columns in their notebooks under the same key words that headed the word sorts. Word study notebooks are a good place to record any other word study activities as well. You might ask students to choose 5 to 10 words to use in thoughtful sentences and coach them through the elaboration process described in the Write and Draw Routine on page 60. Or, have your students practice sorting at home and use the homework form in the Appendix.

3. **Brainstorms:** Ask students to brainstorm other words that contain the same feature and record their brainstorms in their word study notebooks. For example, when studying complex consonants at the end of words, ask students to brainstorm other words that rhyme with a target word that you identify. For example, *latch, patch,* and *hatch* all rhyme with the key word *catch* in sort 42. Be sure to initiate the brainstorm with words that have rhymes that are spelled the same way. This activity can even turn into Word Study Scattergories where students get a point for each brainstormed

word not already on the word sort list. See the activities section of Chapter 6 in *WTW* for more details about Scattergories.

4. **Speed Sorts:** Have students time themselves with a stopwatch as they sort their words into categories. After obtaining a baseline speed, have them repeat the sort several times and try to beat their own time. Repeated, timed speed sorts help students internalize spelling patterns and develop automatic word recognition.

5. **Word Hunts:** Word hunts help students see the connection between reading and spelling. Have students search through books they have already read to find additional exemplars of complex consonants. Students should record the words they find in the proper column in their word study notebook and share them with their group.

6. **Dictated Sentences:** Tell your students that you study spelling patterns so that they can read and spell. Prepare a sentence that contains several of your word study words. Read the sentence to your students and have them write it. Give them feedback about their spelling and mechanics.

7. **Blind or No-Peeking Sorts:** A blind or no-peeking sort should only be done after students have had a chance to practice a word sort several times. Students work together and take turns calling out a word without showing it; one student calls and the other student points to the category it should go in. Both partners then check the word card to see if they were right. No-peeking blind sorts can be conducted as no-peeking writing sorts as well.

8. **Games and Other Activities:** Additional sorts for complex consonants can be found under Diphthongs and Complex Consonants on pages 378 and 393 in the Appendix of *WTW*. The activities section at the end of Chapter 6 describes a Jeopardy Game for *tch* and *ch*. You can download ready-made card games called Take-A-Card that highlight the complex consonants *tch/ch* and *dge/ge* from the *WTW* CD-ROM. There is also a Take-A-Card game for the silent consonants *gn*, *kn*, and *wr*.

9. **Assessment:** Spell Check 6 assesses student mastery of triple *r*-blends and triple digraph-plus-*r*-blend clusters at the beginning of words. Spell Check 7 assesses student mastery of hard and soft C and G as well as *ce*, *se*, and *ve* word endings. Spell Check 8 assesses student knowledge of when to use *tch* versus *ch*, and when to use *dge* versus *ge* at the ends of words.

SORT 36   SILENT BEGINNING CONSONANT SORT *KN, WR, GN*

Students in the within word pattern stage will invariably encounter words spelled with silent consonants. Some have already been included in the earlier vowel pattern sorts in this supplement—*know* was included in the *ow* pattern for the long *-o* sound in sort 20, and *knew* appeared in sort 21 with the *ew* pattern for the long *-u*. But encounters with silent consonants, up to this point, have been incidental. Sort 36 explicitly lays out three categories of silent consonants for direct instruction. Bolded words can be used as key words to head up each category. The bolded words are the most frequently occurring words in the category. Begin by reading and discussing the words and their meanings, paying particular attention to the asterisked homophones. Some students may be totally unfamiliar with the words *knoll, wreath,* and *gnaw,* so think about how you will bring those words to life in advance. Oddballs include two homophones (*rap, ring*), to contrast with their silent partners (*wrap, wring*).

Introduce this sort by establishing the headers and key words, or present it as an open sort and let students discover the categories.

kn	*wr*	*gn*	*oddball*
knife	**wrong**	**gnat**	rap*
knack	wrap*	gnaw**	ring*
known	wreck		
knot*	wrist		
knob	wreath**		
knit	wrinkle		
knight*	wren		
knee	wring*		
kneel			
knelt			
knead			
knoll**			

*homophones
**likely unknown

Demonstrate, sort, check, reflect, and then **extend** as usual by following the standard weekly routines previously described.

More Difficult Words: (4) *knowledge, knowing, writer, written.*

SORT 37   TRIPLE *R*-BLENDS *SCR, STR, SPR*

Students are already familiar with the s-blends *sc, st,* and *sp,* so you might want to begin by writing some words on the board to contrast these easier two-letter blends with their more complex three-letter cousins. For example, you might contrast *sc* words like *scott, scare,* and *scat* with some *scr* words in this sort like *scrape* and *scream.* Likewise, you might compare *st* words like *stop, step,* or *star* with some of these *str* words like *strong, straight,* or *string.* Words starting with *sp* (*spot, speech, spit*) might be contrasted with the *spr* words in this sort (*spring, spray, sprout.*). Starting in this way will guide your students to look carefully at these beginning consonant elements and to listen for the presence of the *r* in the triple blends. You might even count the phonemes in two- and three-letter blends by underlining each letter that goes with each sound. The word *squirrel* is a challenging oddball in which to count phonemes—even if you just stick to the *squ* blend. Do you come up with /s/ + /k/ + /w/ ? Add the next part of the word and you get /s/ + /k/ + /w/ + /r/—something akin to a quadruple blend! The word *squirrel* is included as an oddball here because the *squ* is an "odd" three-letter blend and because it anticipates sort 38.

Once your students are accustomed to looking carefully at these blends, introduce the sort with the key words and direct your students' attention to what is the same and what is different among the *scr, str,* and *spr* blends. Then, **demonstrate, sort, check, reflect,** and **extend** as usual by following the standard weekly routines previously described.

scr	*str*	*spr*	*oddball*
screen	**strong**	**spring**	squirrel
scram	straight	spray	
scrape	strange	spruce**	
scratch	stretch	spread	
scrap	strict		
scream	string		

stripe
struck
strength
stress
strut
strap
stream

**word meaning likely unknown

More Difficult Words: (8) *script, stride, scribe, scroll, stroll, sprawl, sprout, strewn.*

SORT 38   CONSONANT DIGRAPHS-PLUS-*R*-BLENDS AND *SQU* (*THR, SHR, SQU*)

Remind your students that digraphs are two letters that represent one sound. Since the digraphs *th* and *sh* are already familiar to within word pattern spellers, you might begin by contrasting these easier two-letter digraphs with their more complex three-letter digraph-plus-*r*-blends. For example, you might contrast *th* words like *though, thank,* and *thing* with some *thr* words in this sort like *through, three,* and *thrill.* Likewise, you might compare *sh* words like *sheep, shed,* or *shut* with some of these *shr* words like *shrimp, shred,* or *shrink.* You will probably want to contrast the number of phonemes represented in these digraphs and digraph-plus-*r*-blends: *th* represents just one sound whereas *thr* represents two (/th/ + /r/). Revisit the oddball *squirrel* from the previous sort and ask your students to brainstorm other *squ* words. They will probably come up with many of the words in this sort. Starting in this way will guide your students to look carefully at these beginning consonant elements and to listen for the presence of the two sounds in the digraph-plus-*r*-blends (/th/ + /r/; or, /sh/ + /r/) and three sounds in the *squ* blend (/s/ + /k/ + /w/).

As always, be sure to take the time to read and discuss these words, paying particular attention to the asterisked homophones. Word sets like *throw, threw, thrown; shrink, shrank, shrunk,* and *squish, squash* present convenient opportunities to work in lessons on verb tense. The meaning of the double asterisked words may be unfamiliar to your students so you will need to discuss them. After bringing these words to life, introduce the key words, then **demonstrate, sort, check, reflect,** and **extend** as usual by following the standard weekly routines previously described. You simply must read *Shrek* (Stieg, 2002) to your class and make it available for word hunts.

thr	*shr*	*squ*
three	**shred**	**square**
thrill**	shrink	squawk**
throw	shrank	squint**
throne*	shrunk	squish
thrown*	shriek	squash
threw*	shrimp	squeeze
through*		squirt
thrifty**		squeak
threat		squirm**

*homophones
**likely unknown

More Difficult Words: (2) *thrive, shrewd.*

SPELL CHECK 6
ASSESSMENT FOR BEGINNING COMPLEX CONSONANT CLUSTERS

This assessment is presented in a writing sort format and checks for correct spelling of complex consonant clusters at the beginning of words; specifically, triple blends (*scr, str, spr,* and *squ*) and consonant digraphs-plus-*r*-blends (*thr, shr*). All of the 21 words assessed have been studied before in sorts 37 and 38. Say each word clearly and ask your students to write the word in the box labeled with the complex consonant cluster that matches. For example, if you call the word *straight,* students would write *straight* in the sixth box labeled with *str* at the top, since the word *straight* is spelled with the triple-*r*-blend *str.* If you are grading this Spell Check, give one point for writing the word in the correct category and another point for the correct spelling of the entire word.

Call out the words in the following order and use each word in a sentence to make sure your students understand what word you mean. There are two homophones in this assessment so meaningful sentences are crucial. Say each word once, use it in a sentence, and then say it again:

   1. squeeze, 2. straight, 3. threw*, 4. spring, 5. shrink, 6. screen, 7. strong, 8. spray, 9. squirt, 10. scrape, 11. through*, 12. shrank, 13. scream, 14. three, 15. shred, 16. string, 17. spruce, 18. thrill, 19. stripe, 20. scrap, 21. stress

Allow time for students to reorganize their words if needed. Students may want you to repeat the sentences for the homophones *threw* and *through* to make sure they have them in the right order. Student answer sheets will look like this:

1. *squ*	2. *thr*	3. *shr*
squeeze	threw*	shrink
squirt	through*	shrank
	three	shred
	thrill	

4. *scr*	5. *spr*	6. *str*
screen	spring	straight
scrape	spray	strong
scream	spruce	string
scrap		stripe
		stress

*homophone

SORT 39   HARD AND SOFT *C* AND *G*

When the sound of *c* is pronounced /k/ and the sound of *g* is pronounced /g/, they are called hard *c* and hard *g.* When the sound of *c* is pronounced /s/ and the sound of *g* is pronounced /j/, they are called soft *c* and soft *g.* The hard sounds of *c* and *g* occur when followed by *a, o,* or *u.* The soft sounds of *c* and *g* occur when followed by *e, i,* or *y.* This "rule" holds up pretty well and students will get a lot of mileage out of knowing it—not only for reading and spelling words in the within word pattern stage, but also for reading and spelling much harder words later on. *Get* and *give* are oddballs but they occur so frequently they are easy to remember.

Be sure to read and discuss the meanings of these words before introducing the sort. Discuss the homophones *gem, gym, cent,* and *cell.* Even though *sent* and *sell* are not included in this sort, be sure to discuss them and even write them on the board or overhead so that students can see how the homophone partners for *cent* and *cell* are spelled. You might remind students that most homophones are differentiated by their long-vowel pattern, but *cell* and *sell*, *cent* and *sent*, are differentiated by their initial consonant. Also discuss the meaning of the word *gist*, which will likely be unfamiliar to most students.

It is important to sort these words in two ways: (1) by hard and soft consonant sounds at the beginning, and (2) by the vowels that follow the consonant. The first way of sorting teaches students the terminology and shows them how to pay attention to the "softness" or "hardness" of the beginning consonant sound. The second way teaches students to focus on the vowels that follow the consonants. Be sure to have your students sort these words both ways.

To sort by hard and soft consonant sounds, have your students put all the *c* words that start with a /k/ sound in one group and all the *c* words that start with an /s/ sound in another group. Then have students sort all the *g* words that start with a /g/ sound in one group and all the *g* words that start with a /j/ sound in another. After students get the hang of this you can have them sort *c* and *g* words simultaneously, sorting them into two groups corresponding to "hard" and "soft" sounds. The sort will look something like this:

Hard *c*	Soft *c*	Hard *g*	Soft *g*
card	**city**	**gave**	**giant**
code	center	golf	gem*
cart	circle	guess	gym*
cub	circus	guest	gentle
calf	cell*	guide	ginger
	cent*		gist**
	cycle		

*homophone
**likely unfamiliar meaning

To teach students that vowels determine the "hardness" and "softness" of the beginning consonant, have them sort *c* and *g* words according to the vowels that follow them. *C* and *g* words followed by *a, o,* and *u* can be sorted in one group; *c* and *g* words followed by *e, y,* or *i* can be sorted in another group. Again, after they have learned to look for these vowels, students can sort *c* and *g* words by the ensuing vowels simultaneously. Then the sort will look something like this.

Hard			*Soft*	
card	code	cub	city	center
cart	golf	guess	circle	cell
calf		guest	circus	cent
gave		guide	giant	gem
			ginger	gentle
			gist	
			cycle	
			gym	

After reading and discussing the words, introduce the lesson by demonstrating how to sort by the hard and soft sounds of the initial consonants, as previously described. Then, **demonstrate, sort, check, reflect,** and **extend** this basic word sort by following the standard weekly routines previously described. Help your students form generalizations as they reflect on this sort by asking them what vowels follow the hard *c* and the hard *g*, and what vowels follow the soft *c* and soft *g*.

More Difficult Words: (3) *gulf, guard, garden.*

SORT 40   *-CE, -VE, -SE*

In this optional sort, different word endings that include a final *-e* will be compared to focus students' attention to the sound of the final consonant, particularly the /s/ sound of *ce* endings and the /z/ sound of *se*. Words ending in *ve* are included for contrast and to teach students that all English words that end in /v/ also end in *e* (except *LUV* diapers!).

This is a straightforward pattern sort and might be introduced as an open sort. Before introducing it, read and discuss the words, paying particular attention to the homophones *piece* and *peace*. Ask if anyone knows of another word that sounds just like *sense* that has a different meaning, and hence, a different spelling pattern. You might want to add the homophone *since* to the *ce* column. (The word *since* was used in sort 22.)

There are two words included with the *se* word endings that do not have the /z/ sound at the end like the others do (*loose, sense*). Go ahead and sort these two with the *se* endings since this is a pattern sort, but see if your students can spot them. Discuss the spelling and meaning of the word *loose* in contrast to the word *lose*, which does end in a /z/ sound spelled with the *se* ending. To help them remember the spelling of *loose*, ask students if they know any words that rhyme with *loose*. Write down their brainstorms under the word *loose*: *goose, moose*, and *caboose* may be volunteered and a quick study of their sound and spelling pattern will help students differentiate *loose* from *lose*.

-ce	-ve	-se
chance	**move**	**please**
prince	leave	tease
dance	twelve	choose
fence	glove	cheese
piece*	solve	loose**
peace*	prove	wise
bounce	shove	sense*
France		
pounce		
glance		

*homophones
**oddballs by sound of ending

SPELL CHECK 7
ASSESSMENT FOR HARD AND SOFT *C* AND *G* AND WORD ENDINGS *-CE, -SE,* AND *-VE*

This assessment is presented in a writing sort format and checks for correct spelling of hard and soft *c* and *g* at the beginning of words and the word endings *ce, se,* and *ve*. All of the 20 words assessed have been sorted in sorts 39 and 40. Copy and enlarge page 104 for all students you wish to participate in the Spell Check. Say each word clearly and ask your students to write the word in the box labeled with the correct beginning consonant sound in the top row, or the box labeled with the correct word ending in the bottom row. For example, if you call the word *France*, students would write *France* in the third box labeled with *ce* at the top, since the word *France* is spelled with the *ce* ending. If you are grading this Spell Check, give one point for writing the word in the correct category and another point for the correct spelling of the entire word.

Call out the words in the order presented below, and use each word in a sentence to make sure your students understand what word you mean. There are two homophones included in this assessment (*gym* and *peace*), so meaningful sentences are critical. Say each word once, use it in a sentence, and then say it again:

1. twelve, 2. calf, 3. please, 4. city, 5. France, 6. guess, 7. leave, 8. giant, 9. loose, 10. peace*, 11. circle, 12. card, 13. cheese, 14. glove, 15. dance, 16. choose, 17. gym*, 18. fence, 19. gave, 20. prove

Allow time for students to reorganize their words if they need to. Students may want you to repeat the sentences for the homophones *peace* and *gym* to make sure they have spelled the right one. Student answer sheets will look like this:

1. **Hard *c* or *g***	2. **Soft *c* or *g***	
calf	city	
guess	giant	
card	circle	
gave	gym	

3. *-ce*	4. *-se*	5. *-ve*
France	please	twelve
peace	loose	leave
dance	cheese	glove
fence	choose	prove

SORT 41   *DGE, GE*

In most single-syllable short-vowel words that end with a /j/ sound, the final phoneme is spelled *dge (lodge, ledge, bridge, badge, fudge)*. Long vowels, ambiguous vowels, and the letters *r, n,* and *l* indicate the *ge* spelling (*cage, lounge, large, binge, bulge*). This stable state of affairs calls for a good old-fashioned sound sort. Sort by vowel sound—short versus long versus vowel plus *r, l,* or *n*.

Short-Vowel Sounds	Long-Vowel Sounds	Vowel + r, l, or n
edge	**age**	**large**
badge	stage	charge
ridge	rage	surge**
fudge	cage	bulge**
judge	huge*	range
lodge		change
bridge		sponge
ledge		plunge
dodge		
hedge		
pledge		

*the word *huge* was used in sort 10 as an exemplar for the long *-u* sound
**meanings likely unknown

Demonstrate, Sort, Check, and Reflect

Help your students form generalizations by prompting them to articulate what is the same and what is different about words within and across categories. **Compare,** and then, **declare.**

Extend

Look for the *WTW* CD-ROM and check out the Take-A-Card game that features complex consonants *dge* and *ge*.

SORT 42   *TCH, CH*

The same principle illustrated in sort 41 works for the /ch/ sound at the end of words. When you hear a short-vowel sound, use *tch*, unless you hear an *r, l,* or *n* before the final /ch/, in which case you use *ch*. When you hear a long-vowel sound, always use *ch*. The high-frequency words *rich, much, which,* and *such* are exceptions and must be remembered.

Begin with a pattern sort first (*tch, ch*) and then sort the *ch* group by vowel sounds. Either way gets you to this:

tch	ch		r, n, l + ch	oddball
catch	reach	couch	porch	which*
witch*	roach	pouch	torch	rich
pitch	screech		gulch	much
sketch	coach		bench	
fetch	beach		branch	
match			crunch	
hutch				
switch				

*homophone

NOTE: *coach, beach, reach,* and *which have been used in earlier sorts.*

More Difficult Words: (2) *French, speech.*

SPELL CHECK 8
ASSESSMENT FOR COMPLEX CONSONANT CLUSTERS *DGE/GE* AND *TCH/CH*

Review sorts 41 and 42 by sorting them by sound and pattern. Students should see that *tch* and *dge* are associated with short vowels while *ch* and *ge* go with long vowels. Words where the middle vowel is followed by *r, l,* or *n* work similarly.

This writing sort checks for correct spelling of the complex consonants *dge, ge, tch,* and *ch* at the end of words. All of the 20 words assessed have been sorted in sorts 39 and 40. Say each word clearly and ask your students to write the word in one of the boxes labeled *Short Vowel, Long Vowel,* or *Vowel + r, l,* or *n.* For example, if you call the word *lodge,* students would write *lodge* in the first box labeled *Short Vowels,* since the word *lodge* is a short-vowel word so it takes the *dge* spelling. If you are grading this Spell Check, give one point for writing the word in the correct category and another point for the correct spelling of the entire word.

Call out the words in the following order and use each word in a sentence to make sure your students understand what word you mean. Say each word once, use it in a sentence, and then say it again. Feel free to add some exceptions if you like; students can write them across the bottom.

1. change, 2. catch, 3. stage, 4. badge, 5. bench, 6. screech, 7. rage, 8. judge, 9. gulch, 10. pitch, 11. cage, 12. porch, 13. charge, 14. mulch, 15. roach, 16. lodge, 17. coach, 18. pledge, 19. sketch, 20. strange

Allow time for students to reorganize their words if needed. Answer sheets will look like this:

1. **Short Vowels**	2. **Long Vowels**	3. **Vowel** + *r, l,* or *n*
catch	stage	change
badge	screech	bench
judge	rage	gulch
pitch	cage	porch
lodge	roach	charge
pledge	coach	mulch
sketch		strange

kn	*wr*	*gn*
knife	**wrong**	**gnat**
rap	knack	wreck
known	wrist	knot
gnaw	ring	wrap
knob	knit	wren
wring	knight	knoll
kneel	knelt	knee
wreath	wrinkle	knead

Words Their Way: Word Sorts for Within Word Pattern Spellers © 2004 by Prentice-Hall, Inc.

scr	*str*	*spr*
screen	**strong**	**spring**
strange	spray	scram
strut	strap	strict
stress	scream	scrap
spruce	scrape	string
stripe	struck	spread
scratch	stream	straight
stretch	strength	squirrel

thr	shr	squ
three	**shred**	**square**
shrink	squawk	throne
squint	threw	shrank
through	squish	shrunk
squash	shriek	squeeze
thrill	shrimp	squirt
squeak	threat	squirm
thrifty	throw	thrown

Spell Check 6 Sorts 37–38 Beginning Complex Consonant Clusters

1. squ	2. thr	3. shr

4. scr	5. spr	6. str

Soft *c*	Hard *c*	Soft *g*
Hard *g*	city	card
giant	gave	center
circle	code	gem
gym	golf	circus
cart	guess	cell
cub	gentle	guest
cent	calf	guide
gist	cycle	ginger

-ce	-ve	-se
chance	**move**	**please**
prince	tease	leave
glove	choose	dance
fence	shove	loose
glance	piece	cheese
peace	wise	solve
bounce	prove	sense
France	twelve	pounce

Name _____

1. Hard *c* or *g*

2. Soft *c* or *g*

3. -ce

4. -se

5. -ve

dge	**ge**	**r, l, n + ge**
edge	**age**	**large**
badge	stage	charge
range	ridge	rage
cage	surge	bulge
lodge	fudge	huge
change	judge	bridge
ledge	sponge	dodge
hedge	plunge	pledge

tch	*ch*	*r, l, n + ch*
catch	**reach**	**porch**
coach	bench	witch
pitch	beach	torch
gulch	pouch	which
sketch	screech	roach
fetch	match	branch
couch	crunch	hutch
rich	switch	much

Words Their Way: Word Sorts for Within Word Pattern Spellers © 2004 by Prentice-Hall, Inc.

Spell Check 8 Sorts 41–42 Complex Consonant   Name _____
Clusters dge/ge and tch/ch

1. Short Vowels	2. Long Vowels	3. Vowel + R, L, or N

SORTS 43-44

High-Frequency Words and Contractions

NOTES FOR THE TEACHER

Sorts 43 and 44 take us on a detour into the world of high-frequency words and contractions. Up to this point we have included phonetically irregular high-frequency words in word sorts as oddballs. For example, the word *said* was examined along with other long -*a* words that have the *ai* pattern such as *paid* and *wait*. A word like *said* becomes memorable in word sorts because it stands alone in contrast to the many words that work as the pattern would suggest. It is also memorable because students have seen it so often when they read. But there are also some words that students need to write frequently that have not been heretofore included in these weekly lessons. An example of this is the word *because*, which students often spell in their own inventions as BECUZ, BECALZ, or BECAWS. Sort 43 targets many of the high-frequency words that start with the unaccented syllable *be-* (*be*cause, *be*lieve, *be*hind). These words are contrasted with another group of high-frequency words that start with the unaccented syllable *a-* (*a*gain, *a*bout, *a*cross).

Sort 44 focuses on some high-frequency contractions, words that collapse two or more words by removing some letters and replacing them with an apostrophe. Students need to understand how contractions work so they know where to put the apostrophe when they write, and so they can understand the meaning of contractions when they read. Easier contractions were examined in the letter name-alphabetic supplement (*I'm*, *he's*, *she'll*). In sort 44 we examine more advanced contractions distilled from the combination of adverbs (*where, there, here*), relative pronouns (*this, that, who, what*), and the like, with helping verbs (*is, have, will*). Sort 44 presents contractions in groups: the *not* group, the *is* group, the *have* group, and the *will* group. The objective is for students to learn that the apostrophe marks the spot where the letters were removed.

In addition to the sorting activities recommended throughout this supplement, we suggest that you follow our guidelines for the study of high-frequency words as outlined at the end of Chapter 6 in *WTW*. To summarize, the routine we suggest there includes: (1) discussing each word to identify trouble spots as well as familiar chunks, (2) using a self-corrected pretest, followed by (3) the self-study method (look, say, write, and check), and (4) spell checks.

Follow the Standard Weekly Routines for word sorts as described in all previous sorts:

- **Demonstrate, Sort, Check, Reflect, and Extend**
- **Repeated Work with Word Sorts**

- Writing Sorts and Word Study Notebooks
- Change-O
- Word-O
- Speed Sorts
- Word Hunts
- Dictated Sentences
- Blind or No-Peeking Sorts
- Games and Other Activities

Assessment

To assess students' mastery of these high-frequency words and contractions, ask them to spell, read, and write the words. Spell Check 9 assesses students' knowledge of high-frequency words in a cloze format using antonyms and synonyms. Spell Check 10 assesses student mastery of more advanced contractions with another cloze procedure in which students write the contraction in the blank provided.

SORT 43   HIGH-FREQUENCY WORDS STARTING WITH *A-* AND *BE-*

Sort 43 targets high-frequency words that start with an unaccented syllable. Because the first syllable is unaccented or unstressed, the vowel is reduced to an /uh/ sound as in "*uh-bove*" for *above,* and "*buh-cause*" for *because.* Fortunately the vowels in the accented or stressed syllable sound and look more familiar—the *way* of *away* and the *fraid* of *afraid* are spelled with the familiar CVV and CVVC long-vowel patterns studied earlier. The same phenomena exists in the "buh" group and the second syllable is sometimes a complete word: the *side* in *beside,* or the *long* in *belong,* for example. It is important to guide your students to recognize what they already know in these high-frequency two-syllable words to move them into the next level of word study where they will examine syllables and affixes in detail.

Demonstrate, Sort, Check, and Reflect

Prepare a set of words to use for teacher-directed modeling. You might make a transparency to cut apart and model sorting on the overhead projector. Display the words and begin by asking the students to read over them to see if there are any they do not know or understand. Since most of these words are adverbs, prepositions, conjunctions, or abstract verbs, these words are hard to discuss. Their meaning is not concrete. To get the conversation going you might find all the words having to do with "location" such as *above, below, ahead,* and *behind.* Or, ask students to find some words that could describe a person (*afraid, alive, asleep*). After discussing the words, go ahead and display the headers *a-* and *be-,* then model sorting the words by their beginnings. After sorting all the *a-* words together and all the *be-* words together, read through all the words in a single column. You might want to clap to the rhythm of syllable stress and talk about how the second syllable is accented. See if anyone can find a long vowel in any of the stressed syllables and identify the pattern. Here is the sort:

a-	*be-*
ago	begin
away	because
again	before

around	between
about	behind
alive	belong
ahead	become
above	beside
across	believe
afraid	below
asleep	began

Extend

After your students have sorted their own word cards and have recorded them in their word study notebooks, ask your students to underline the second syllable of words that are words by themselves. Here is a list of words that contain words in their second syllable:

ago, away, around, alive, ahead, across, asleep
because, belong, become, beside, below

SPELL CHECK 9
ASSESSMENT FOR HIGH-FREQUENCY WORDS STARTING WITH A- AND BE-

This assessment is presented in a cloze format and students must recall 10 high-frequency words that will complete each sentence and write them correctly in the blanks provided. The first five words are prompted by an antonym (opposite) clue in a cloze sentence format. The second five words are prompted by a synonym or definition in a cloze sentence format. If you are grading this assessment, give one point for the correct word choice and another point for its correct spelling. The sentences, and their answers, are as follows:

Antonym Cloze:
1. The opposite of *above* is (*below*).
2. The opposite of *before* is (*after*).
3. The opposite of *asleep* is (*awake*).
4. The opposite of *ahead* is (*behind*).
5. The opposite of *dead* is (*alive*).

Synonym Cloze:
6. Another word for *scared* is (*afraid*).
7. To do something *one more time* is to do it (*again*).
8. Another way of saying *to start* is to (*begin*).
9. To *get from one side of the street to the other*, you must go (*across*).
10. If I *trust* that you are telling me the truth, I (*believe*) you.

SORT 44   CONTRACTIONS

Sort 44 presents 23 contractions in groups: the *not* group, the *is* group, the *have* group, and the *will* group. These words are boldfaced to be used as key words or column headers. The objective is for students to learn that the apostrophe marks the spot where the letters were removed.

Demonstrate, Sort, Check, and Reflect

Display the headers *not, is, have,* and *will*. Tell your students that contractions are like compound words with one or more letters removed. Use your finger to cover the *o* in the word *not* and explain that if you took the *o* out of *not,* you could put an apostrophe there instead to mark the place where you removed the letter. Put the word *couldn't* under the header *not* and ask a student to show you where the *o* was removed. Use the same procedure for *is*. Cover up the *i* and explain how you could take a shortcut in writing by removing the *i* and putting an apostrophe in its place. Put the word *who's* under the header *is* and ask someone to show you where the *i* was removed. The words *have* and *will* are a bit more complicated, because the first two letters are removed instead of just the vowel, but you can use the same procedure.

Not	Is	Have	Will
couldn't	who's	could've	they'll
wouldn't	there's	would've	that'll
aren't	here's	should've	this'll
weren't	where's	might've	who'll
shouldn't	what's		she'll
doesn't			he'll
hasn't			you'll

Extend

See if your students can apply their skill with apostrophes to read dialect dialogue in books like *The Talking Eggs* (by Rober D. San Souci), or *Pink and Say* (by Patricia Polacco). Both of these books make heavy use of apostrophes to represent dialect in the dialogue.

SPELL CHECK 10
ASSESSMENT FOR CONTRACTIONS

In this assessment, students read a sentence that contains two underlined words that could be combined and written as a contraction. Students simply write the contraction in the space provided. If you are grading this assessment, each answer is worth one point. The sentences and answers are as follows:

1. They will come to my house for dinner. (*They'll*)
2. Who is going to the party? (*Who's*)
3. She could have won the prize if she had signed her name. (*could've*)
4. They are not the ones who did it. (*aren't*)
5. Here is the work that you missed. (*Here's*)
6. You should not forget your homework. (*shouldn't*)
7. I might have done it differently if I had thought about it. (*might've*)
8. "Who will help me sow the wheat?" asked the Little Red Hen. (*Who'll*)
9. What is five plus three? (*What's*)
10. He does not have enough money to go to the movies. (*doesn't*)

a-	*be-*	ago
begin	again	because
away	between	around
before	believe	about
alive	become	belong
ahead	beside	across
below	asleep	afraid
began	behind	above

Spell Check 9 Sort 43 High-Frequency Words Starting with *a-* and *be-*

Name _____

Antonym Cloze

1. The opposite of *above* is _____.

2. The opposite of *before* is _____.

3. The opposite of *asleep* is _____.

4. The opposite of *ahead* is _____.

5. The opposite of *dead* is _____.

Synonym Cloze

6. Another word for *scared* is _____.

7. To do something *one more time* is to do it _____.

8. Another way of saying to *start* is to _____.

9. To *get from one side of the street to the other,* you must go _____.

10. If I *trust* that you are telling me the *truth,* I _____ you.

Not	Is	Have
Will	couldn't	who's
could've	they'll	wouldn't
there's	would've	that'll
aren't	here's	should've
this'll	weren't	where's
might've	she'll	doesn't
he'll	hasn't	you'll
shouldn't	what's	who'll

Words Their Way: Word Sorts for Within Word Pattern Spellers © 2004 by Prentice-Hall, Inc.

Spell Check 10 Contractions   Name _____

Write the contraction for the underlined words.

1. <u>They will</u> come to my house for dinner. _____

2. <u>Who is</u> going to the party? _____

3. She <u>could have</u> won the prize if she had signed her name. _____

4. They <u>are not</u> the ones who did it. _____

5. <u>Here is</u> the work that you missed. _____

6. You <u>should not</u> forget your homework. _____

7. I <u>might have</u> done it differently if I had thought about it. _____

8. "<u>Who will</u> help me sow the wheat?" asked the Little Red Hen. _____

9. <u>What is</u> five plus three? _____

10. He <u>does not</u> have enough money to go to the movies. _____

SORTS 45–46

Inflectional Endings for Plural and Past Tense

NOTES FOR THE TEACHER

Although issues of changing the base word to accommodate plural and past tense endings are more suitably addressed in the next stage of word knowledge, the syllables and affixes stage, it is important for students in the late within word pattern stage to acquire a conceptual understanding of the plural endings *s* and *es,* and of the past tense *ed,* as meaning units that can be added to base words to indicate number or tense. Students in the late within word pattern stage may still spell these inflectional endings phonetically, as in BEACHIS for *beaches,* or JUMPT for *jumped.* Although students may use these grammatical forms correctly in their speech, they are not aware of them as orthographic meaning units or morphemes in print. Since late within word pattern spellers are reading and writing many words with inflectional endings, it is fitting that they learn the conventional spelling of the two most frequently occurring inflectional endings, plurals and past tense. Changes to the base word to accommodate these endings, such as consonant doubling, dropping the final *e,* or changing the *y* to *i* will not be addressed here. These more complicated conventions are addressed in the next *WTW* book on sorts for spellers in the syllables and affixes stage.

The letter *s* or *es* is added to a base word to indicate "more than one." For example, if you eat one *chip,* you will eat two *chips.* If you make one *wish,* it will be for three *wishes.* The inflectional endings *s* and *es* are stable and are always spelled the same way regardless of pronunciation. Students need to be shown how this works. Most of the 25 words presented in sort 45 have been presented in earlier sorts in this supplement in the singular form. As a result, it will be easy for students to find and underline the base word in these inflected forms. After identifying the base word, students sort by word endings (*s* or *es*) to discover the spelling trends in the base word that indicate *s* or *es.*

The easiest way to build a conceptual understanding of *ed* as an invariant orthographic unit that tells us that something has already happened in the past is to have students categorize words with *ed* endings by their ending sounds. Having students sort words with various *ed* sounds leads them to the realization that no matter how we pronounce it, we primarily use *ed* to indicate that an event has happened in the past. In sort 46, students sort words ending in *ed* by sound, then they circle the part that tells that the event already occurred in the past. Again, most of the words in sort 46 have been introduced in previous sorts without the inflection. The point of sort 46 is to introduce students to the invariance of the past tense morpheme *ed,* regardless of how it sounds. Follow the Standard Weekly Routines suggested for previous sorts.

SORT 45   PLURAL ENDINGS *S* AND *ES*

Begin by passing out the student sorts and asking them to underline the base word in each rectangle before they even cut them up. If the term *base word* has not come up before, you will need to lay some conceptual groundwork. After students have underlined the base word, discuss what is left over—the *s* or *es*. Tell your students that adding an *s* or *es* to a base word tells us there is more than one. You may need to elaborate on this point by comparing one inch to two inches; one girl to two girls, and so on. Remind your students that they have sorted most of these words in the singular form in an earlier sort.

Once your students have underlined the base word and they understand that the *s* or *es* added to the end of the base word indicates more than one, ask them to sort their word cards by their plural endings—*s* or *es*. This sort should result in two columns that look like this:

+ *s*	+ *es*
eyes	inches
plants	stitches
pieces	boxes
places	taxes
pages	bushes
girls	dishes
months	wishes
houses	classes
badges	glasses
	dresses
	lunches
	flashes
	roaches
	leeches
	bosses
	riches

Ask your students: *How do you know when to add* s *and when to add* es? After taking on a few hypotheses for discussion, have your students sort the +*es* group by the final letter(s) of the base word, then ask that question again. Is there a reoccurring pattern in the base word of the +*es* group? They should notice that all of the base words end in *sh*, *ch*, *s*, or *x*. If students volunteer the final letter *h* instead of *sh* or *ch*, direct their attention to the word *month* in the +*s* column, then ask them to revise the hypothesis.

Demonstrate, sort, check, reflect, and **extend** as usual by following the standard weekly routines previously described.

SORT 46   THREE SOUNDS OF THE PAST TENSE ED

If your students have been in the within word pattern spelling group throughout this book and they have worked with you using the previous sorts, they may recognize just about every one of these words because they have seen them before without the *ed* ending. Tell your students that they are studying these words again because they have all been changed to the past tense by adding an *ed* to the end. It is important that you spend some time discussing the concept of past versus present tense by using some of the words in this sort in contrasting sentences with and without the *ed*. For example, you might play Yesterday and Today, with the words in this sort. To play Yesterday and Today, choose a word from the sort, take off the *ed,* and then use the base word in a sentence using the present tense for *today*. With the word *started*, for example, you could take off the *ed* and generate the sentence, "Today I *start* my yoga class." Next, put the *ed* back on and say, "Yesterday, I *started* my yoga class."

As soon as your students understand the difference between past and present tense, have them categorize their *ed* words by their ending sounds.

Demonstrate, Sort, Check, and Reflect

Display the headers /d/, /id/, and /t/ and tell your students that the letters in the middle of the slash marks indicate the final sound in these words: Some words end in a /d/ sound; in others, the *ed* forms a second syllable and the second syllable sounds like /id/. Some words end in a /t/ sound.

Hold up the word *picked* and pronounce it, giving special emphasis to the last sound. Demonstrate how you would put the word *picked* under the /t/ to match its final sound. Next, hold up the word *prayed* and pronounce it, emphasizing the final sound. Model how you would place the word *prayed* under the /d/ since you hear a /d/ sound at the end of the word. Finally, hold up the word *waited* and pronounce it with special emphasis on the second syllable, /id/. Demonstrate how you would categorize the word *waited* under the /id/. Continue on in this manner, gradually involving your students in the decision-making, sorting process.

After your demonstration, pass out the student sort sheets and make sure everyone can read each word. After your students cut up their word cards, ask them to sort the words under the three sounds of *ed*: /d/, /id/, and /t/. Their sorts should end up like this:

/d/	/id/	/t/
prayed	**waited**	**picked**
rained	loaded	jumped
snowed	needed	walked
screamed	melted	bumped
turned	started	missed
mailed	twisted	passed
cleaned	handed	dressed
yelled	dusted	asked

Extend

After your students have sorted their past tense *ed* words by ending sounds, have them circle the part of each word that tells it already happened in the past. They should all circle the *ed*. Help your students reflect on this sort by calling on students to summarize what they learned. Hopefully, they all will learn that the past tense morpheme *ed* is always spelled *ed* no matter how it sounds.

Extend this sort further by having your students go on a word hunt for other words ending in *ed*. Ask them to add their words to their word study notebooks in the proper columns. *Good Hunting, Blue Sky* (by Peggy Parish) is chock-full of *ed* words!

SPELL CHECK 11
BASE WORD + INFLECTION: PLURAL
AND PAST TENSE ENDINGS

The assessment for plural and past tense endings is conducted in a cloze sentence format. Students read a sentence that contains an underlined word and then complete the sentence by filling in the blank with the proper inflection.

The Spell Check for plurals requires students to change the underlined word from the singular to the plural form by adding an *s* or *es*. Students write the inflected word in the blank provided.

The Spell Check for past tense requires students to change the underlined word from the present tense to the past tense by adding *ed*. Students write the inflected form of the word in the blank provided.

Tell students to read each sentence carefully and look for the underlined word. Tell them to complete each sentence by changing the underlined word to the plural form or past tense and writing it on the blank provided. Each answer is worth one point. There are 10 plurals and 10 past tense items. The sentences and answers may be found below:

Plural Check (Based on Sort 45)

1. I have one <u>plant</u> but she has two (*plants*).
2. My brother's <u>class</u> has two gym (*classes*) on Fridays.
3. Each new <u>month</u> gets us closer to the (*months*) ahead.
4. She needed a new <u>dress</u> but she shouldn't have bought five new (*dresses*)!
5. The treasure hunt took them from <u>place</u> to <u>place</u> until they had been to all of the (*places*) they could possibly go.
6. I cannot see you as clearly with one <u>eye</u> shut as I can with both (*eyes*) open.
7. We moved from <u>house</u> to <u>house</u> until we had lived in five different (*houses*).
8. He grew <u>inch</u> by <u>inch</u> until he had grown three (*inches*).
9. One <u>box</u> was red and another <u>box</u> was blue, but all of the (*boxes*) had ribbons.
10. He hid behind one <u>bush</u> then ran to the (*bushes*) on the other side of the lawn.

Past Tense Check (Based on Sort 46)

1. Her teacher told her to <u>ask</u> nicely so she (*asked*) as nicely as she could.
2. It might <u>rain</u> again today. Last night it (*rained*) two inches.
3. I hope it will <u>snow</u> tonight. Last year it (*snowed*) on Valentine's Day.
4. The snow will <u>melt</u> when the sun comes out. Last time it (*melted*) before noon.
5. He can <u>jump</u> higher than anyone on the team. He (*jumped*) seven feet at the last meet.
6. She can really <u>yell</u> loudly. She (*yelled*) so much at the game that she lost her voice.
7. The girls won't <u>start</u> in the race this week. Last week they (*started*) before the gun went off.
8. The workers <u>pick</u> apples all fall. Last fall they (*picked*) 2,000 barrels of apples.
9. They <u>load</u> the apples onto trucks. Last year they (*loaded*) 500 trucks.
10. Mrs. Smith <u>walks</u> everyday. Last week she (*walked*) 10 miles.

SORT 45   Plural Endings *s* and *es*

+**s**	+**es**	dishes
eyes	inches	stitches
boxes	bushes	places
pages	wishes	classes
glasses	riches	dresses
girls	taxes	houses
bosses	roaches	flashes
leeches	months	badges
pieces	plants	lunches

/d/	/id/	/t/
prayed	**waited**	**picked**
jumped	loaded	rained
needed	snowed	walked
screamed	melted	bumped
turned	missed	started
passed	mailed	twisted
cleaned	handed	dressed
dusted	yelled	asked

Spell Check 11 Part I: Plurals   Name _____
(Based on Sort 45)

*Read each sentence carefully and look for the underlined word. Complete each sentence by changing the underlined word to the **plural form**. Write the **plural form** of the word in the blank provided.*

1. I have one <u>plant</u> but she has two _____.

2. My brother's <u>class</u> has two gym _____ on Fridays.

3. Each new <u>month</u> gets us closer to the _____ ahead.

4. She needed a new <u>dress</u> but she shouldn't have bought five new _____!

5. The treasure hunt took them from <u>place</u> to <u>place</u> until they had been to all of the _____ they could possibly go.

6. I cannot see you as clearly with one <u>eye</u> shut as I can with both _____ open.

7. We moved from <u>house</u> to <u>house</u> until we had lived in five different _____.

8. He grew <u>inch</u> by <u>inch</u> until he had grown three _____.

9. One <u>box</u> was red and another <u>box</u> was blue, but all of the _____ had ribbons.

10. He hid behind one <u>bush</u> then ran to the _____ on the other side of the lawn.

Spell Check 11 Part II: Past Tense   Name _____
(Based on Sort 46)

*Read each sentence carefully and look for the underlined word. Complete each sentence by changing the underlined word to the **past tense**. Write the **past tense** of the word in the blank provided.*

1. Her teacher told her to <u>ask</u> nicely so she _____ as nicely as she could.

2. It might <u>rain</u> again today. Last night it _____ two inches.

3. I hope it will <u>snow</u> tonight. Last year it _____ on Valentine's Day.

4. The snow will <u>melt</u> when the sun comes out. Last time it _____ before noon.

5. He can <u>jump</u> higher than anyone on the team. He _____ seven feet at the last meet.

6. She can really <u>yell</u> loudly. She _____ so much at the game that she lost her voice.

7. The girls won't <u>start</u> in the race this week. Last week they _____ before the gun went off.

8. The workers <u>pick</u> apples all fall. Last fall they _____ 2,000 barrels of apples.

9. They <u>load</u> the apples onto trucks. Last year they _____ 500 trucks.

10. Mrs. Smith <u>walks</u> everyday. Last week she _____ 10 miles.

124

SORTS 47–48

Long -*a* and Long -*i* Homophones

NOTES FOR THE TEACHER

By now your students have encountered many homophones in the previous 46 sorts and hopefully these words have been brought to life through group discussions and extension activities such as Write and Draw and Homophone Dictionaries. *Words Their Way* has many suggestions for using homophones in vocabulary instruction and lists many children's book titles that play on their word meanings. Homophones are fun to study because of the way meaning is altered by a simple change in the vowel pattern.

Sort 47 presents 52 homophones that all have the long -*a* sound. Some of the words have been sorted before but many of them are new. Most of the long-vowel patterns presented will be familiar, but a few new long -*a* patterns will crop up as well. We recommend that these words be sorted first by pairs that sound alike. Students will most likely know the meaning of at least one word in the pair, so it will be easy for them to learn the meaning of the other one by contrast. For example, students are apt to know the meaning of the word *pain*, but may not be as familiar with the meaning of the word *pane*. By discussing the meaning of the word *pane* in contrast to the other *pain*, students will easily associate the window with the CVCe spelling. You might have them draw pictures on their word cards to cue new meanings.

Sort 48 presents another set of homophones, all containing the long -*i* sound. Again, we recommend sorting these words out into pairs first so that students can discuss their meanings. The patterns for the long -*i* homophones are much more varied and there will be many new ones to consider. Additional homophone games are described in *WTW*. We especially like Homophone Rummy, which is why we include 52 homophones in sort 47. The directions to that game may be found in Chapter 6 of *WTW* and additional words for more homophone card games may be downloaded from the *WTW* CD-ROM.

SORT 47 LONG -*A* HOMOPHONES

Since there are so many words in this sort, you will probably want to introduce it over a two-day period. Begin by passing out the student sorts and asking them to cut them up and put all the words that sound alike together. Once the pairs are together, have students tell you the word meanings they do know and you can tell them the meanings of any they do not. Have your students draw little pictures on the homophones they do not know so they can remember them. Once this is accomplished, have your students sort the homophones by vowel patterns. There are no headers provided because all but one pattern has been previously taught in earlier sorts in this supplement. Headers are provided below, however, so you can see how the sort should go. If you do want to use headers, look in the Appendix.

Demonstrate

CVCe	ai	ea	ay	ei
mane	main			
bale	bail			
pale	pail			
hare	hair			
made	maid			
pane	pain			
plane	plain			
stare	stair			
pare	pair	pear		
tale	tail			
vane	vain			vein
fare	fair			
waste	waist			
sale	sail			
maze	maize			
bare		bear		
	raise		rays	
ate				eight
			way	weigh
wade				weighed
	wait			weight
daze			days	
stake		steak		
brake		break		
	rain			rein

After your students have completed the sort, ask them if any new patterns came up. Some students may say the *ei* pattern while others may volunteer *eigh*. Some discussion of the silent letters *gh* may help them to broaden their category to accept all of the *ei* words together.

Have students **sort, check,** and **reflect** on the different patterns associated with the different meanings of these homophones. After they have sorted their words several times, teach them how to play Homophone Rummy!

Extend this sort by having your students hunt through the wonderful homophone books listed in *WTW* on page 419. Our favorite is *The King Who Rained* (F. Gwynne).

SORT 48 SHORT AND LONG -*I* HOMOPHONES

Sort 48 will review short and long -*i* sounds and many of the long -*i* vowel patterns studied in the earlier sorts: the CVCe pattern, the *igh* pattern, and a variation of the open-syllable *y* pattern. Some of these homophones will call on students to remember the past tense *ed* as they consider the meanings of the words *sighed, tied,* and *fined.* But there are a few new patterns here, some of them very unusual. See if your students can tell you which ones they are.

Demonstrate

This sort is best introduced as an open sort; or, try introducing it as a Guess My Category activity as described in Chapter 3 of *WTW*. Either way, students start by matching homophones. They will find that some have three words in a set. The following sort displays the long-vowel patterns only:

clime	knight	night			
write	right				
site	sight				
mite	might				
time			thyme		
stile			style		
tide					tied
side					sighed
find					fined
		die	dye		
		lie	lye		
by			bye	buy	
hi	high				
I			eye		
wry			rye		
isle	I'll	aisle			

After students sort, have them **check** and **reflect** on the meanings of these words as well as their spelling patterns. **Extend** this sort with a word hunt in *Amelia Bedelia* and discuss how her misunderstanding of homophones propelled the plot.

stake	tale	fair
maze	wait	mane
bail	pear	stair
made	hair	plane
main	bale	pair
pail	bear	rays
way	ate	eight
pare	pale	hare
pane	plain	steak

Words Their Way: Word Sorts for Within Word Pattern Spellers © 2004 by Prentice-Hall, Inc.

SORT 47-2   Long -a Homophones

rein	sale	waist
break	rain	fare
maize	daze	pain
maid	days	vein
bare	weight	tail
vain	stare	vane
weigh	waste	sail
raise	wade	brake
weighed		

lie	I'll	dye
sight	lye	I
night	thyme	fined
eye	isle	write
might	side	hi
site	style	tide
sighed	time	knight
die	find	buy
by	aisle	high

bye	right	tied
mite	stile	hymn
guilt	him	mist
its	wit	gilt
ring	missed	it's
knit	in	whit
tick	nit	wring
inn	rye	tic
clime	climb	wry

Appendix

Headers for Long and Short Vowels

Short ă	Long ā	Short a
Long a	Short ĕ	Long ē
Short e	Long e	Short ĭ
Long ī	Short i	Long i
Short ŏ	Long ō	Short ŏ
Long ō	Short ŭ	Long ū
Short ŭ	Long ū	
oddball	*oddball*	*oddball*

Vowel Pattern Headers

oddball	*oddball*	*oddball*
_o_e	_u_e	_a_e
_i_e	_ake	_ack
_oke	_ock	_ike
_ick	_uke	_uck
_ook	_oo_	_oa_
_ai_	_ui_	_ee_
_ea_	_ay	_ew
_ue	_ow	_y

Less Common Vowel Pattern Headers and Complex Consonant Cluster Headers

_ild	_igh	_old
_ost	_ind	_air
_ear	_are	_ire
_ier	_eer	_oar
wor_	_ore	_ure
_oi_	_oy	_au_
_aw	_oo_	_al_
wa_	_dge	_ge

More Spelling Headers

kn_	wr_	gn_
scr_	str_	spr_
thr_	shr_	squ_
_ce	_ve	_se
_tch	_ch	

Blank Sort Template

WORD WORK AT HOME

Name _____ Date _____

Cut apart your words and sort them first. Then write your words below under a key word.

_____

_____

_____

_____

_____

_____

_____

_____

_____

_____

What did you learn about words from this sort?

_____

_____

_____

On the back of this paper write the same key words you used above. Ask someone to shuffle your word cards and call them aloud as you write them into categories. Look at each word as soon as you write it. Correct it if needed.

Check off what you did and ask a parent to sign below.
_____ Sort the words again in the same categories you did in school.
_____ Write the words in categories as you copy the words.
_____ Do a no-peeking sort with someone at home.
_____ Write the words into categories as someone calls them aloud.
_____ Find more words in your reading that have the same sound and/or pattern. Add them to the categories on the back.
                    Signature of Parent _____

Words Their Way: Word Sorts for Within Word Pattern Spellers © 2004 by Prentice-Hall, Inc.

Word Sort Corpus

about	black	**bruise**	circle	**creep**	draw
above	blame	brush	circus	crier	drawn
across	**blare**	build	city	**crime**	dream
afraid	**blaze**	built	**claim**	**croak**	dressed
again	blew	bulge	classes	crook	dresses
age	blind	bump	claw	crop	drier
ago	**blond**	bumped	clay	cross	drip
ahead	bloom	burn	clean	crowd	drive
aid	blow	**burr**	cleaned	crown	**drop**
aisle	blue	burst	clear	**crude**	**drought**
alive	**blurt**	bushes	clerk	**cruel**	drove
almost	**blush**	buy	**click**	**cruise**	drown
also	boar	by	**clip**	**crumb**	drum
arch	board	bye	**cloak**	crunch	duck
aren't	**boast**	cage	close	**crush**	dude
around	boat	calf	cloud	crust	due
ask	boil	calm	**clove**	cry	duke
asked	**bold**	came	clown	cub	dune
asleep	**bolt**	camp	club	cube	**dusk**
ate	book	cape	clue	curb	dusted
away	**booth**	card	coach	cure	dutch
badge	bore	care	coal	curl	dye
badges	**bored**	cart	**coarse**	curse	each
bail	bosses	catch	coat	curve	ear
bait	both	caught	**coax**	cute	earn
bald	bought	cause	code	cycle	earth
bale	bounce	cell	coil	dance	east
barb	boxes	cent	coin	dark	edge
bare	boy	center	cold	dawn	eight
base	brain	chain	**colt**	days	enjoy
bath	brake	chair	**comb**	daze	eye
bawl	branch	chalk	come	dead	eyes
beach	**brass**	chance	cook	**deal**	face
bear	brave	change	cool	dear	**fact**
beard	bread	charge	**coop**	death	**fail**
because	break	cheer	core	decoy	faint
become	**breast**	cheese	corn	deer	fair
beef	breath	chew	**cost**	dew	**faith**
been	**breeze**	**chick**	couch	die	**fake**
before	**brew**	child	cough	dirt	**fame**
began	**brick**	**chime**	could	dish	fare
begin	bridge	**chip**	could've	dishes	fast
behind	bright	chirp	couldn't	do	fault
believe	**broad**	choice	count	**dock**	**fawn**
belong	broil	**choke**	**court**	dodge	fear
below	broke	choose	**cove**	doesn't	feet
bench	**brood**	chop	coy	**dome**	fence
beside	brook	**chord**	crab	done	fern
between	broom	chore	**crash**	**doom**	fetch
bike	brought	chose	**crate**	**doubt**	few
bird	**brow**	church	crawl	**dove**	fight
birth	brown	churn	**creek**	**doze**	**file**

film	froze	**grin**	hoist	knob	loss
filth	fruit	**grip**	hole	knock	lost
find	fudge	**groan**	home	knoll	lots
fined	**fuel**	groom	hood	knot	love
fir	**fume**	ground	hook	know	lunches
fire	fur	grow	hoop	**knowing**	**lurch**
firm	**fuse**	growl	hope	**knowledge**	lure
first	**fuss**	grown	horn	known	lurk
fist	gain	**guard**	horse	**lair**	lye
flair	**garden**	guess	hose	**lame**	mad
flake	**gasp**	guest	**host**	**lamp**	made
flame	gave	guide	hot	**lane**	maid
flare	**geese**	gulch	houses	large	mailed
flash	gem	**gulf**	howl	**lark**	main
flashes	gentle	gum	**hue**	last	maize
flaw	germ	**gust**	huge	laugh	make
flea	ghost	gym	hung	launch	mane
flew	giant	hair	hurl	law	march
flier	gift	**halt**	**husk**	lawn	**mast**
flight	ginger	hand	hutch	lay	match
flip	girl	handed	I	lead	**mate**
float	girls	hard	I'll	leaf	**math**
flock	gist	hare	inches	**leak**	**maul**
floor	give	harm	isle	learn	maze
flop	glance	**harp**	jack	**leash**	**meal**
flow	**glare**	**hart**	jar	**least**	mean
flue	glass	hasn't	**jay**	leave	melted
flute	glasses	haul	jeep	ledge	mice
fly	**glide**	**haunch**	**jerk**	leeches	might
foam	globe	haunt	job	**leer**	might've
foil	**gloom**	have	join	less	mild
fold	glove	hawk	joint	**liar**	mind
fond	glue	hay	joke	**lice**	**mint**
food	gnat	he'll	**jolt**	lick	**mire**
foot	gnaw	head	joy	lie	missed
for	**goal**	**health**	judge	life	mite
ford	goat	hear	juice	like	**moat**
forge	gold	heard	jump	**lime**	moist
fork	golf	heart	jumped	load	**mold**
form	good	heat	June	loaded	**mole**
fort	**gorge**	hedge	junk	loaf	months
fought	gown	her	just	**loan**	mood
foul	grain	**herb**	keep	**loaves**	moon
found	**grand**	herd	kick	lock	more
four	**grape**	here's	kind	lodge	most
fourth	grass	hi	knack	**lone**	mouth
fowl	**grave**	high	knead	long	move
frame	gray	**higher**	knee	look	mow
France	**graze**	hike	kneel	**loom**	much
French	great	**hind**	knelt	**loop**	mule
friar	**greed**	**hint**	knew	loose	**mute**
frier	green	hire	knife	**loot**	nail
fright	**greet**	**hive**	knight	**lope**	near
frown	grew	hoarse	knit	lose	needed

nerve	pitch	quite	salt	shrink	**sole**
new	place	**quote**	same	shrunk	solve
next	places	race	**sand**	shut	some
nice	plain	rage	sauce	shy	soon
night	plane	rain	saw	sick	soot
nine	plants	rained	**scale**	side	**sore**
noise	play	raise	**scar**	**sift**	**sought**
none	please	rake	scold	sigh	sound
nook	pledge	range	**scoop**	sighed	south
noon	pliers	rap	score	sight	soy
north	**plop**	**rare**	**scorn**	since	space
note	**plot**	rash	scout	sir	Spain
nurse	plow	**rate**	**scowl**	**sire**	**spare**
oak	ploy	raw	scram	site	speak
oar	**pluck**	**ray**	scrap	**skate**	spear
oat	**plug**	rays	scrape	sketch	**speech**
oil	**plum**	reach	scratch	skin	**speed**
once	**plume**	rear	scream	**skip**	**spice**
ore	plump	rein	screamed	skirt	**spike**
ought	plunge	rich	screech	skunk	**spine**
owe	**plus**	riches	screen	sky	**spire**
owl	point	ridge	**screw**	**slap**	**spite**
pack	pouch	right	scribe	**slate**	spoil
page	pounce	ring	**script**	slave	spoke
pages	pound	**ripe**	scroll	**slay**	sponge
pail	**pour**	rise	**sear**	sled	**spook**
pain	**praise**	**risk**	search	sleep	**spool**
paint	pray	roach	seat	**slice**	spoon
pair	prayed	roaches	sense	**slid**	spot
pale	**price**	road	serve	**slight**	**sprawl**
palm	**pride**	roam	sew	slope	spray
pane	**prime**	roar	**shade**	**slot**	spread
pare	prince	roast	shake	slow	spring
part	prize	**robe**	shape	**slump**	**sprout**
passed	**prompt**	rock	shark	**sly**	spruce
past	proof	rode	sharp	small	**spun**
paste	prove	**role**	shawl	**smash**	spur
pause	**prowl**	roll	she'll	**smile**	**spurt**
paw	**prude**	Rome	**shelf**	smoke	square
peace	prune	**rook**	**shine**	smooth	squash
peach	**psalm**	roost	shirt	snap	squawk
peak	**pump**	root	shook	**snare**	squeak
pear	pure	rose	**shop**	**sneer**	squeeze
pearl	**purge**	rough	shore	snore	squint
peel	purple	**rove**	should	snort	squirm
peer	purr	row	should've	snowed	squirrel
perch	purse	rude	shouldn't	**snuff**	squirt
perk	put	rule	shout	**snug**	squish
pest	**quack**	**rust**	show	soap	**stack**
phone	**quake**	sack	shrank	soar	stage
picked	queen	safe	shred	**sob**	**stain**
piece	**queer**	said	**shrewd**	sock	stair
pieces	quick	sail	shriek	soft	stake
pine	quit	sale	shrimp	soil	**stale**

stalk	stripe	**thaw**	toy	waited	which
stall	**stroke**	there's	**trace**	**wake**	wipe
stamp	**stroll**	they'll	**track**	walk	wire
stand	strong	**thigh**	trade	walked	wise
stare	struck	thin	train	wand	wishes
start	strut	third	**tramp**	want	witch
started	stuck	thirst	tray	**ware**	**woke**
stay	style	this'll	**thread**	wash	wood
steak	such	those	**treat**	wasp	wool
steam	suit	**though**	trees	waste	word
steer	sure	thought	**tribe**	watch	wore
stem	surf	threat	troop	**water**	work
stern	surge	three	**trough**	wax	world
stew	swap	threw	truck	way	worm
stile	swat	thrifty	true	weak	**worse**
stir	**sway**	thrill	trunk	**wealth**	worst
stitches	**swear**	**thrive**	trust	wear	worth
stock	sweep	throne	truth	web	would
stole	sweet	through	try	week	would've
stomp	**swept**	throw	tube	weigh	wouldn't
stone	**swift**	thrown	tune	weighed	**wove**
stood	swim	thumb	turkey	weight	wrap
stool	swirl	thyme	turn	weren't	wreath
store	switch	tide	turned	**whale**	wreck
storm	**swore**	tied	**tusk**	what	wren
stout	**sworn**	**tilt**	twelve	what's	wring
stove	tail	time	twice	when	wrinkle
straight	take	tire	twirl	where	wrist
strange	tale	toad	**twist**	where's	write
strap	talk	toast	twisted	**whew**	**writer**
straw	tall	toil	use	**while**	**written**
stray	**tame**	told	vain	**whir**	wrong
stream	**task**	**tone**	vane	whirl	wrote
street	taste	took	vault	white	yard
strength	taught	tool	vein	who'll	yawn
stress	taxes	tooth	voice	who's	year
stretch	teach	torch	**volt**	whole	**yearn**
strewn	team	tore	vote	why	yelled
strict	tease	torn	**vow**	**wide**	**yoke**
stride	teeth	**touch**	wade	wife	you'll
strike	term	tough	waist	wild	**zone**
string	that'll	town	wait	**wind**	**zoom**